I0809201

The Novel of Crepuscular Universes

THE NOVEL OF CREPUSCULAR UNIVERSES

Essay

Thomas Mann, Robert Musil,
Hermann Broch, Witold Gombrowicz,
Günter Grass, Curzio Malaparte,
Heinrich Böll, L.-F. Céline

Ion Vlad

English translation by Delia Drăgulescu

EAST EUROPEAN MONOGRAPHS, BOULDER, CO
DISTRIBUTED BY COLUMBIA UNIVERSITY PRESS, NEW YORK, NY
2010

EAST EUROPEAN MONOGRAPHS
No. DCCLXIV

Copyright 2010 by
East European Monographs

ISBN: 978-0-88033-663-5

Library of Congress Control Number:
2010923621

All rights reserved

Printed in the United States of America

To my parents
In Memoriam

TABLE OF CONTENTS

Translator's Note ix

Ion Vlad
THE NOVEL OF CREPUSCULAR UNIVERSES
Essay
Thomas Mann, Robert Musil, Hermann Broch, Witold Gombrowicz, Günter Grass, Curzio Malaparte, Heinrich Böll, L.-F. Céline

Introduction to "The Novel of Ideas" xiii

Alternatives Within the Poetics of the Novel 1

The Experiences of Lucidity. The Experiences of Drama 53

The Resources of the Anti-Novel 75

The Remembrance of the Picaresque Novel 91

TRANSLATOR'S NOTE

I need to make a few observations regarding the quotations present in Ion Vlad's book. Given the fact that I was based in Berlin at the time I translated this book, it was very difficult, and at times impossible, to find all the English translations or the original English works mentioned by Ion Vlad. Therefore, I was forced to translate into English the Romanian translations of those references. As regards Musil's *The Man without Qualities*, Ion Vlad used a Romanian edition which translated the complete 1978 Frisé edition, including the posthumous chapters, that is chapters 39-128 of Part III. The English edition I found, although a translation of the Frisé edition, lacks the posthumous chapters and consequently, I translated quotes taken from the respective chapters.

Introduction to "the novel of ideas"

Is there a distinct heraldry of "the novel of ideas"? Is this kind of taxonomy still up-to-date and, even more so, is it still viable within the wide and heterogeneous sphere of narrative types? Can an idiom such as this, "the novel of ideas", really be validated? These are several, undoubtedly non-isolated questions within the framework of acknowledged debates regarding the universal novel from a narrative perspective, or from the standpoint of the narrative forms' poetics. Throughout the following pages, the idea of a *meditation-novel* and/or of a *reflexive novel* crystallized only within the never closed or worn-out space of *reading*. This is the only privilege of the encounter with literature: the reading and the recurrences stimulated by works astonishing due to their open universe.

It can be stated (why not?) that any novel – seen under the genre of totality and polysemy, similar through the adaptation of certain criteria to its nature, morphology and meanings – incorporates various "voices"; the polyphony, the protean nature, the polymorph structure are as many arguments to plead the case of the "total" novel, of the novel of imaginary "macro- and microcosm".

Nevertheless (within the sphere of the novel, the criteria, the solutions and the interpretative instruments are always numerous!), there is a novel of human ontology where meditation, the comments inspired by the evolution of Time (historical and internal) and the specific forms of the reflexive discourse are preeminent. Furthermore, the conclusions of contemporary sciences are the main argument for giving up those prejudices obstinate in declaring a "closed" status of literature, confusing the specific, distinct nature and the identity of a literary work with a sealed territory, impermeable to the (necessary) dialogue with the other areas of knowledge. The old and famous Aristotelian parallel, favorable to "poetry" compared to "history", was not abandoned because *The Poetics* written in the IV century B.C. did not have an arbitrary and exclusivist nature. In reality, the forms of knowledge cooperate and do not annul the communication's distinctive nature, the ontology of each type of world's exploitation, a certain epistemology (see Aristotle, *The Poetics*).

Hence, I quoted the text of Ilya Prigogine and the confession of the two great physicians, the Dane Niels Bohr and the German Werner Heisenberg. Their contribution to modern physics (quantum mechanics) has surprising consonances with literature, and I will give only one indisputably remarkable example: Lawrence Durrell. If for Niels Bohr "the inseparability of the issue of reality from that of human existence" (Prigogine; Stengers, 1997) represents a fundamental topic of his meditation/research, for the author of the quartet dedicated to Alexandria, to its myths and allure, to the human restless passions, the perspective inspired by science is an absolutely passionate one. The confessions found in the extraordinary correspondence with Henry Miller (*A Private Correspondence*) are actually a program, a philosophy of compositional vision, of Time and Space (Lawrence Durrell – Henry Miller, *Une correspondence privée*, Buchet/Chastel, 1963). Just like in the analyses of the *chronotope* carried out by M. M. Bakhtin (the functions, the significance, the preeminence of time and its action in relation to the narrative space), Lawrence Durrell travels a course ever more connected to Einstein's theory, extrapolated and extended to the contributions of quantum mechanics.

The symphonic poem of the cycle made up of *Justine, Balthazar, Mountolive* and *Clea* (1957-1960) is illuminated by a radically changed concept (the term is totally justified!) of Time, thus annulling the visions of Proust or Virginia Woolf; the positioning into abyss has the mission of emphasizing the revolt against *memory-time*. It is the question of what the writer defines as "heraldic existence" in one of his letters addressed to the American novelist Henry Miller (1936), evoking Paul Valéry and the poet's fascination for a *heraldic ideogram*, a universe of thinking, and the "mathematics" of spirit and creation. Furthermore, in one of the most impressive confessions about his literary work, Durrell viewed the narrative quartet as a "poem of relativity" (William Faulkner, *Romanciers au travail*, Gallimard, 1967; p. 194). Einstein's concept of relativity becomes for Lawrence Durrell the solution of a *continuum* beyond Bergson's suggestions (focusing on a time segment); the literary references are expressive, but the most important one is James Joyce ("Joyce reached Homer") to underline the value of certain works that clearly transgress the Bergson effect. In contrast, Durrell advances Einstein's concept of time, in a "stereoscopic" narrative of a "stereophonic" nature (Ibid., pp. 192-193). The quartet's explicit poetics is not disinterested in the topic of these initial considerations; in *Balthazar*, the intervention of the auctorial author is direct: "[...] I'm trying to finish a novel in four layers, whose form is based on the theory of relativity. / Three parts space and one part time, the recipe for this inexorable fusion" (Lawrence Durrell, *The Alexandria Quartet*, London, Faber and Faber, 1962; p. 14). Such an experience requires of course a different epic construction, a different narrative morphology, and that which had to be demonstrated: a novel presided by idea and by the meditation on its poetics, through the discourse's nature and intellectual supremacy. Because Durrell's quartet was unimaginable without such references to a temporal and spatial perspective, without precedent in Proust's works inspired by Bergson's philosophy. The interferences; the insertion of different narrative forms such as the diary, the letters; the intervention of the auctorial author (the idea of the mental recreation of the entire city and its delirium in the memory of the narrator and his actors); the meta-novel (*Balthasar*, *Clea*); the formula of reviving and reinterpreting an initial narrative module and its transformation into an epic continuum require – I believe – a different approach to the novel's structure; this is a novel of permanent meditation, of continuous tension, of *re-creating* the spatial-temporality. Hence, the idea of the imagined effect and of a perception differently prepared and forewarned.

Within rhetoric, the narrative's forms represent "a privileged territory" (The μ Group, *Retorica generală*, Bucharest, Univers, 1974), also because the narrativity permits numerous generalizations that constitute the nucleus of certain interpretations. The authors state that "the narrative sign is the relation between the story that tells the story and the told story" (Ibidem); namely: the discourse and the story. The story becomes a fundamental term, implying the trauma, the syntactic game of the trauma's organization, the imaginary interpretations of the universe etc.; however, the processes take place at the level of the discourse and not at the surface of the narrative description. Hence, the nature of the representations, *the ambiguity of the narrative communication* and the totally different nature of certain types of novels where the relations between "story" and "discourse" are blurred by the use of the solutions typical of the reflexive novel. The difficulty is also generated by the often confusing narrator's points of view and by the heteroclite nature of the types of discourses: confessional, epistolary, and sensitized by the elements of the visual, of film and painting, of the non-verbal universe. Their assimilation is characteristic to this type of novel and the interferences at the level of the intertextuality, of the referents' proliferation liberates the novel from any restraints. The epic time and the spatial vision are visibly shaped and influenced by a different world and existential approach.

Ilya Prigogine and Isabelle Stengers claim that the XX century started "with a twofold explosion" (Prigogine, Stengers, 1997): relativity and quantum mechanics, two fundamental fields that created certain essential theoretical schemes; thus, one should not be surprised by the fact that scientific research changes or radicalizes the perspectives, reaching a new vision on evolution and existence. A new ontology is difficult to imagine in the absence of the sciences' "directives", and the writer *is born* in a differently evaluated time, re-measured through movement and irreversible processes, through the effect of the entropy within the human and, implicitly, creative space. The cognitive pathos of literature and especially that of the novel is acknowledged from the standpoint of the literary discourse's specificity and of the literature's rationality of being an explorer of existences. The two authors evoke Einstein in order to proclaim a new approach and an outlook fired by the lights of science: "The mystics struggled *to feel* this world as an illusion; as regards Einstein, he wants *to demonstrate* that it is nothing but illusion, the only truth being a transparent and intelligible universe, cleansed by everything that affects the human existence – the nostalgic or painful recollection of the past, the fear for or the faith in the future" (The authors' emphasis, Ibidem).

This "nostalgic and painful recollection" of time and of the world projected into a future time could serve as an emblematic statement for the novel's role and for the mission assumed by an impressive number of novelists throughout the century that has just ended. It would probably be advised, before proceeding with other considerations related to the narrative and the poetics of the novel/novels, to quote a fragment from the work of a novelist obsessed with the creation act and with the condition of the XX century writer: "When the XIX century collapsed on the front of the Armageddon, the old restrictions blew up. The demoniac artist that had dominated the century had contributed to the containment of the past to the same extent as the state people, the militarism, the great finances, the industrialists and the agitators who had paved the road to disaster. The 1914 war seemed to mean something; anyway, it was the climax of something already surpassed. And, in reality, it opened vast new prospects. Via its destroying actions, it created channels for discharging the immense new energy. The interval between the First and the Second World War was artistically productive. During this period, when the world was about to be shaken off for a second time, I started taking shape. It was a difficult period especially because one could only trust oneself, one's own strengths. The society, torn by all sorts of dissensions, offered the artist even less support and encouragement than in the time of Van Gogh. The very existence of the artist was being questioned. But didn't this threat menace any human existence?" (Henry Miller, *Plexus*) There is no doubt about it: the novel remains, unwavering and with an often betrayed determination (the new French novel), an attempt at exploring and examining – under the species of ontology – the human destiny; it is an act of immense responsibility for the creator, and the incentive of the American novelist, witness of History and of the declines, is meaningful: "Stop working hard and start creating! Because creation is a game and the game is divine!" (Miller, *Plexus*).

Fully agreeing with M. Bakhtin, I believe that *the game* initiates the history of the great narrative with the works of Rabelais, *Gargantua* and *Pantagruel*, thus marking the beginning of the *grotesque realism* and of the *carnivalesque*, of the genre's protean and extensive structures. Furthermore, the great Russian esthetician considers that the defining characteristic of the Rabelaisian experience is the development of the grotesque and carnivalesque as undeniable and durable signs of "the degradation". To quote Bakhtin: "The main characteristic of the grotesque realism is *the degradation*, that is the transfer of everything that is sublimely spiritual, ideal, abstract to the material-physical level, to the level of the earth and body, indissolubly connected to one another" (M. Bakhtin, *François Rabelais şi cultura populară în Evul Mediu şi în Renaştere*, Bucharest, Univers, 1974). Bakhtin, the author of the well-known concept of *chronotope*, also recommends a certain interpretation of "the grotesque image" from the perspective of time: "The relation with *time*, with *evolution* is a necessary constitutive (determinant) characteristic of the grotesque image" (Author's emphasis, Bakhtin, 1974).

To a certain extent, Rabelais's novel constructs under the sign of *ambivalence* the entire process of articulation and compositional organization of the great novel for which the heterogeneity and the eclectic nature represent the two poles of evolution and transformations.

***

As early as 1952-1953, M. Bakhtin represented in his historical retrospective (literary history was always privileged by the great theoretician and historic of French culture) *the forms* (the genres) as *heterogeneous structures*, protean through their absorption force and receptivity to other types of the non-verbal discourse. In *Speech Genres*, the researcher also examines the literary individual forms (species) by comparison to other forms of linguistic communication. Beyond the advanced taxonomy ("primary genres" - epistolary literature, daily dialogue, and "secondary genres" - *the novel*, dramatic literature, theatre as performance, the scientific or philosophic discourse etc.), Bakhtin claims that we witness a *dynamic interaction*, open and emphasized by the regime of the intertextuality, decisive for the evolution and vitality of the narrative forms (M. Bakhtin, *Esthétique de la creation verbale*, Gallimard, 1984/2000; pp. 265-267). The theoretician's statements regarding *the choice* of "the genre" are interesting; the factors are numerous, but among them there are the phenomena detected by the creator, the novelist's "partners" (for the novel) recruited from the symptomatic manifestations of reality, of their significances. On a different occasion, Bakhtin examines the open and receptive nature of the novel as "inserted" form, that is "the inclusion in its structure of various genres, both literary and extra-literary (familiar, rhetorical, scientific, religious etc.). In principle, any genre can be introduced in the construction of the novel [...]." (Bakhtin, *Probleme de literatură şi estetică*, Bucharest, Univers, 1982).

Finally, in the same context, the researcher emphasizes the great permeability of the novel, *shaped* (as regards its structure and inner organization) by combinations often surprising given the mutations and metamorphoses of the genre's physiognomy: "Each of these genres has its own verbal-semantic forms of assimilating the diverse aspects of reality" (Bakhtin, 1982). An expert on the history of narrative forms, Bakhtin knows very well that from Rabelais and especially from Cervantes onwards the novel covers decisive phases culminating, as regards the very history of the form, with the experience of the XVIII century novel. Laurence Sterne, Fielding, Richardson or Diderot prepare the completion of the process of assimilating and absorbing certain types of expressions and of verbal discourse (such as the journal, the correspondence, the confession, the memoirs, the pamphlet, the essay) in a *whole* which becomes the novel in its modern acknowledgement.

Jacques Derrida referred to the inner *strength* of writing, meaning *creation* within a tension indissolubly connected to the nature of the imagined structures (cf. J. Derrida, *L'écriture et la difference*, Éditions du Seuil, 1967; pp. 11-13). In general, the theory of forms (and especially the poetics of narrative forms) emphasizes the dynamics of certain inner relations, the narrative structures' constant evolution and adaptation to new requirements and to new circumstances for the formation of the writers and for their vision of the world. Fundamental is the representations' dimension, the conscience of creation within a restless and endless journey of the thought and the outlook on the world. The creative act and the lucidity of interpretation, that uninterrupted or ever-abandoned guard is just like Jacob's fight against that very Someone, remaining strong and unyielding, snatching his blessing, a sign of the mankind's strength of fighting... The novelist is compelled to keep his energy and inner force, while projecting and realizing that supreme tension of creation and of converting the world in the representations of his imagination, in vast fictions called novels!

***

"As field of license, the novel does not know any limits, any laws. Its nature requires it to break them all and to give in to any temptation which urges its fantasy. Maybe the gradual development of the novel throughout the XIX century does not accidentally correspond to the progressive rejection of the rules that determine the form and content of literary genres" (Roger Caillois, *Romanul politist; jocul si drama*, in "Secolul 20", no. 7, 1968). The essay is dedicated to the crime novel, to its traditions and morphology, to the rigors and "geometry" of this narrative genre which, today, proves to be extremely rebellious against the rules mentioned by Caillois. The advanced observations are however interesting; they are part of the introduction to the magazine's analysis: a theme issue of *Secolul 20*. The brilliant essayist and researcher emphasizes that it is an inevitable process of rebellion against the rules (a "general tendency to anarchy", says Caillois), a process of casual, unpredictable development of forms (in theatre and poetry as well), a permanent course of adaptations and changes, of syntheses and "interpolations" (Bakhtin). Specifically, as regards the nature of epic forms, an important part is played by the reference system, the intertextuality and the sensibility of the novelist; the narrator has long ceased to remain just a "cold" observer, miraculously breathing life over the earth... The novelist is a character determined to interpret and analyze, like a scientist in a scholarly convergence of instruments, where anatomy and physiology, the very tense study of ideas and the conscience of a deep human crisis generate the defining directions of the XX century novel.

There is an extraordinary stream of factors, signs of an often convulsive universe; there is the world's cosmic movement and the infinite universe of the existences placed under "surveillance" by the novelist – a creator of worlds and a creator of emotions, of destines, of large panoramas within the chronicle-novel, or a creator of structures geometrized through rigor and reflexive lucidity. Despite the narrative forms, there are defining invariables, such as the narrative fiction, the nature and forms of representation, the narrator's points of view, the syntheses generated by the protean structure, by the genre's absorbent structure etc. One of its characteristics is undoubtedly *the inner, rational and emotional strength*. Umberto Eco also examines the novel from the perspective of the mechanisms that produce emotions, an *ars combinatoria* created by a "scholar" who cleanses and filters everything: "Chemistry is never mistaken. There also is a *chemistry of emotions* and, according to an ancestral tradition, an ingenious plot is always an ingredient generating emotions" (Umberto Eco, *De superman au surhomme*, Bernard Grasset, 1993; p. 13). It is one of the rationales and the vitality sign characteristic to the genre. Unimaginable outside "the history" of certain existences, the novel remains an eternal *story*, creating within the territory of fiction, narrating dramas, describing events, drawing portraits and inviting the reader to take a flight within the space of the imaginary.

If the novel is always a story, we accept that its history means a narration of events capable of fascinating, captivating and stimulating the system of representations created by the reader. Aristotle's *Poetics*, aforementioned in these prolegomena, defines (tragedy is the superlative, but the statements are also valid for the epic forms) "imitation" via action; therefore, the main terms are the conflict and the plot, the characters and their evolution, the nature of their *catharsis* (Aristotle, *The Poetics*). Unadjusted, they can be confirmed in relation to the narrative forms as well, suggesting a true narrative strategy meant to surprise, move and influence "the reader". Aristotle does not neglect any important, universally valid element within the narrative structure and within the reference system that is part of the effect produced by the narrative forms. Given that to narrate is almost synonymous with imagining fictitious worlds, it can be inferred that the epic event represents a system of structural referents, of temporal connections, a communicative mechanism and, of course, multiple actions of narrating and creating *histories* (cf. Jacques Moeschler; Anne Reboul, *Dictionar enciclopedic de pragmatică*, Cluj-Napoca, Ed. Echinox, 1999).

Paul Ricoeur considers that as verbal composition, the story is, in Aristotelian terms, *mythos*. Namely, it is created as a story-narration, accompanied by the plot (intrigue), a script based on a scholarly strategy of the development and outcome or, as stated by the famous hermeneutist, it is a "setting-in-the-plot" (Paul Ricoeur, *De la text la acțiune. Eseuri de hermeneutică*, Cluj-Napoca, Ed. Echinox, 1999). On the "surface" examined by Paul Ricoeur there are the various forms of the story, as archetypal nucleus, as primary text. Thus, the novel's forms are established because, like the other texts born from narrative enunciation, the novel is story and therefore, it is *history*: "Between living and narrating, a distance is hollowed out, no matter how small. Life is lived, history is narrated." (Ricoeur, 1999). The narrative forms' relation with the temporal dimension, within the phases of the genre's evolution, does not rule out beyond certain experiences the presence of time as accounted *time*, emphasizing the fact that the story establishes a time of the narrator, a time of the events and a time of the reader. Paul Ricoeur underlines: "Everything that is narrated happens within time, requires time, develops in time, and that which develops in time can be narrated. Moreover, maybe a temporal process can only be recognized as such if it can be narrated one way or the other" (Ibid.).

Within the sphere of "artificial narrative" (Teun Van Dijk, "Action, action description and narrative", in Umberto Eco, *Lector in fabula*, Éditions Grasset & Fasquelle, 1985; p. 87), there are also the actions attributed to the potential worlds, worlds favored by the vision and complexity of the narrative, where the characters, the individual destinies, create the potential world as a "cultural construction" (Van Dijk, 1985, pp. 157-158). Within the open game of unlimited freedom, the reader ("the empiric reader" of course) chooses the type of composition, building a *world* from the narrative fiction (cf. Umberto Eco, *Şase plimbări prin pădurea narativă*, Ed. Pontica, 1997).

The novel is known to be the expression of a cultural development; the act of story-telling has broadened to include multiple forms, epic "histories" or, as described by Paul Ricoeur, "the fiction stories" brought up on the narrative nucleus of a story more often situated beyond literature. I find the reading of a novel and the understanding of its forms' evolution to be more accurate in Bakhtin's interpretation expressed in one of his most fascinating books: *Problems of Dostoevsky's Art*. Terms famous in the narrative field (narrative polyphony, heterogeneity etc.) become more convincing thanks to the analysis advanced by the Russian researcher. Bakhtin examines the history of the genre starting with Rabelais, Cervantes and Grimmelshausen, the Iberian picaresque novel and the XVIII century novel, without leaving aside the feuilleton-novel (Eugène Sue, Alexandre Dumas). Thus, he creates a *history* which, probably for the first time, is legitimized by the real evolution, and not by the evolution of the literary historian having restrictive geographical and cultural prejudices. I believe that Bakhtin's merit is that of having reasoned the narrative's heteroclite nature through the rediscovery of the archetypal sources of the novel itself, and not only of the story. Furthermore, Bakhtin examines the forms of the myths, of the fairytale, of the *carnivalesque performance*, of the game of rendering the world into a carnival via unpredictable and often unusual combinations of elements of grotesque, comic, Platonic dialogue, or the Boccaccio-style "serialized" story. A similar open, polymorph and protean universe, where the gothic, the adventurous or the philosophic novels etc. join one another, justifies and legitimizes the XX century novel and its forms; among them, the *reflexive novel* is tempted not only by meditation but also by the inexhaustible and imaginative game projected on the signs and manifestations of these worlds of the novel (cf. M. Bahtin, *Problemele poeticii lui Dostoievski*, Bucharest, Univers, 1970).

As a matter of fact, the XX century novel, and especially the novel of open meditation on the most innovative forms, as well as the novel of the world's great myths (the South-American novel, the American novel, the Russian novel, and mainly the narrative which emerged after the disappearance of cultural Stalinism) have discovered the most surprising forms of expression. They enriched the narrative discourse, easing the supremacy of the *allegory-novel* and of the *parabola-novel* (in Europe, the Italian narrative represented by Italo Calvino or Dino Buzzati etc.), as well as the supremacy of the novel with reflexive expressions (Robert Musil, Hermann Broch, Hermann Hesse, Elias Canetti etc.). Essentially, the abovementioned "carnivalesque" means, among other things, the permeability and availability of the genre to the proliferation of voices, of the forms of the characters' participation in a space of meditation on the human condition and its chances. I am sure that the "temporal horizon" about which wrote the Romanian Lucian Blaga in "The Trilogy of Culture" ("Besides a spatial horizon, conscience also has a temporal horizon", Lucian Blaga, *Trilogia culturii*, Bucharest, E.L.U., 1969) contains the perspective open to reflection and the human configuration of a world that draws the lines of its existence.

The history of the modern novel (I concur with the interpretation given by Milan Kundera in *The Art of the Novel* and in *Testaments Betrayed* to the concept of a "modern novel" initiated by Rabelais, settled as destiny by Cervantes and consolidated as regards its vision and forms through the experience of the XVIII century novel) secures, in an gnoseological and ontological understanding, a specific epistemology, a permanent "time" of "realism". However, this "eternal" realism (the Aristotelian *mimesis*) develops whimsically contradicting the ancient teachings and betraying frequently (and at the same time polemically) the initial relations of this "veracity" in and via fiction. An alerted researcher of narrative, Jacques Dubois, reiterates the expression of the novel seen "as a vast organic entity", not forgetting to point out the accidental and unpredictable development, through continuous mutations and metamorphoses, of a genre drawn by the *re-creation*, in paradoxical forms, of the world's complexity and plurality. Jacques Dubois states that the novel discovers the continents of utopia, of fantasy, of poetry and, I would add: myth and magic, reflexivity. Because "realism" "is reborn in each era under new forms that revolutionize our vision and understanding of reality, as well as the poetry of the works" (Jacques Dubois, *Les romanciers du réel*, Éditions du Seuil, 2000; p. 13). A new poetics of the novel and a radical change of paradigm decide a reevaluation and a recreation of the narrative forms through the revelation of the universal, not necessarily to the disadvantage of individuality/singularity; numerous and often disconcertingly unpredictable changes have crossed the structure of the genre starting with the XIX century when realism, in its classical organization (individual destinies, typologies, the study of society, the exploitation of History and of the indissoluble relations with the individual and society: Balzac, Flaubert, Dickens etc.), consolidates its program. The great novels of the XX century (Franz Kafka, Proust, Joyce, Virginia Woolf, Italo Svevo) decide the fate of the novel although each of the named writers applies solutions and discourse types with often opposing references. The tension of the ideas often identifies itself with new ways of taking on the world and of proclaiming the role of a rational Narrator, having however to wear the masks predestined by the laws of the new narrative. The view of the novelist presides, surveys, a witness and a creator of worlds, a tragic and obsessive presence of acute sensibility, condemned to perceive everything. The temporal relations; the narrative space; the self-referentiality; the meditation and the depth of observation; rational, clinical; the intertextuality; the dissipated levels; the dissolution of certain categories considered unyielding; the role of the epic event and the subjective projection of the narrator are all changing elements, some of which substitute variants, while others initiate a new way of investigating and speaking about the human nature and about its existential purpose.

Thus, beyond the undergone experiences, some essential for the evolution of the novel as instrument of exploring consciences and investigating existence, the novel continues to be, within the genre of permanence, *epic history, story* and therefore, a creation for the ever more prepared reader to detect meanings and signs of potential worlds beyond the fable. This is a world "read" by the creator and recreated by its receiver, recipient of this "reading"-interpretation! (cf. Richard Rorty, *Heidegger, Kundera şi Dickens*, in "Pragmatism si filosofie post-nietzscheana", Bucharest, Humanitas, 2000). Therefore, the novel is an indirect answer to the torturing questions of the historical being attacked and inhabited by anxieties, by the darkest premonitory signs. It is a known fact that throughout the history of narrative, the phases dedicated to and decided by the personality of certain novelists (Rabelais, Cervantes, Grimmelshausen; the XVIII century novel, the gothic novel, Balzac, Dickens, Flaubert, Dostoevsky, Tolstoy, Gogol, Goncearov, Turgenev; the novel of the early decades of the XX century) are marked by radical changes of vision, by literary and world-perceiving doctrines. The novel's destiny and the adventure of its forms, ever more diversified and heterogeneous, are determined by interferences and by the interaction of numerous phenomena: ideological, philosophical, social etc. Above everything else there is *History*, the human history projected on the dynamics of experiences, on their repercussions on the individuals and implicitly on the collective conscience.

Maybe the writers' confessions, the information provided by the *poetics* employed and assumed by the novelists are able to communicate and explain the factors generating options regarding the writing, the artistic conscience, the canon recognized or deciphered through the interpretation of the actual literary texts. A symptomatic model for the novelists formed during the decades following the First World War is James Joyce, and the proclamation of his role in the novel's restructuring is significant. The abandonment of Proust's formula, not without consequences for revolutionizing the vision and the temporal perception, the abandonment of the mechanics of psychology are the result of the extremely strong and even brutal impact of Joyce's *Ulysses*. One of the most illustrative examples for the implications of the encounter with Joyce's work is Hemingway. For the American novelist, Joyce's *influence* essentially imposes a *model* perceived and re-identified in the works of other novelists of his time. Furthermore, the great story-teller finally speaks in the name of his generation: "[...] the influence of his work had transformed everything, allowing us to liberate ourselves from all constraints" (Faulkner, 1967, p. 135). The names of other writers who Hemingway judged the authors of works he had honored during his literary formation and apprenticeship are also significant; thus, a true "course" of narrative history was projected: Stendhal, Flaubert, Mark Twain, Turgenev, Tolstoy, Dostoevsky, Chekhov, Maupassant, Kipling and above all: Shakespeare. And while the latter contains in his works the reasons of the great novel, Dostoevsky quintessentially expresses the novel, *the modern novel* situated beyond any chronology or specific forms.

It would maybe be appropriate for me to note that as regards the inter-war Romanian narrative, the most significant tendencies were organically linked to the novel of classic realism, with the infusion of solutions typical of the analytical novel; other directions taken by the contemporary European narrative were more uncommon and rather isolated. As the literary critic Eugen Lovinescu noted, the Romanian experiences were synchronized with the European experiences, and the professionalization of the genre was ever more evident; the exceptions were connected to the unforgettable role of the story (Mihail Sadoveanu) and to the "authentic" experiment (Mircea Eliade, Anton Holban, Max Blacher, Mihail Sebastian, Octav Suluțiu etc.). Relatively singular were the attempts to produce literature where the experiment and the self-referentiality acquired a new path, through the employment of the ellipse, the digression, the fragmentation and the narrative fraction (C. Fântâneru), whereas H. Bonciu and Ion Biberi acquired influences close to the Joyce model.

Nevertheless, the absolute model, definitely fixed in the writers' conscience, invariably remains Dostoevsky. I do not think that there is a novelist from the great family of the writers who had influenced the evolution of the genre not to have uttered the name of the modern novel's creator. Here, the idiom "modern novel" defines the totalizing status of a form where supple, open forms converge in extraordinary combinations, always moving and generating new syntheses. And Dostoevsky creates the new novel, makes it exist as supreme model, no matter what solutions, discourse nature or poetics are assumed. It is simply the novel as form of the existence and manifestation of the world in a language common to all and, in spite of this characteristic, a language inaccessible to the other explorers of the world.

Dostoevsky makes the existence of the *synthesis-novel* possible, of the novel where all the voices and all the methods tried before acquire an unparalleled dimension: it is the novel as expression of existence. When a novelist like Henry Miller adopts in his trilogy *The Rosy Crucifixion* the solution of the auctorial narrator defined through a confessional discourse with numerous bookish and generally cultural references (writers, essayists, philosophers etc.), he rather pathetically confesses his fidelity to the absolute model of Dostoevsky: "I thought about my friend Lou Jacobs who used to take his hat off each time he passed by one of Shakespeare's statues. What I offered Dostoevsky was more than a salute or a bow. It was rather a prayer, I was asking him to unlock the mystery of the revelation. What a common, plain face he had! A Slavic face, the face of a thug. The face of a man who can go unnoticed in a crowd [...]. I was sitting motionless, as usual, trying to uncover the mystery of the being that was hiding behind the features' pasty mass. But I could only make out pain and stubbornness. A man who obviously had favored the life of the poor, a man who had just come out of prison. I got lost in contemplation. Finally, I could only see the artist, the tragic, astounding artist who had created an authentic pantheon of characters, of individuals that hadn't ever existed before him and wouldn't exist ever again after him; each of them more real, stronger, more mysterious, more inscrutable than all the crazy tsars and all the cruel and vile popes put together." (*Plexus*).

***

I once analyzed the opinions of Milan Kundera on the novel and on the condition of the novelist (cf. Ion Vlad, *În labirintul lecturii*, Cluj-Napoca, Ed. Dacia, 1999), as well as the paradigm built by the Czech writer: the establishment of the modern world in the relation Descartes – Cervantes (see Kundera, *The Art of the Novel*, Perennial Classics, 2000), determining the configuration of a vision guided by rationality, the logic of ideas and the settlement of a narrative universe completely "rationalized" by the view of the genius. Maybe it is exactly on this paradigm that the novel's poetics can be legitimized, presided and protected by the *idea* - a novel of the meditation on the human condition, not lacking philosophical reflection; on the contrary, by recreating it in the animated world of the novel seen as history of destinies and as original, unmistakable spatial-temporality. The Czech writer induced the discovery of new inner forces of the genre and of polyvalences, sometimes neglected or placed on inferior positions. A true leitmotiv of the two volumes of essays signed by Milan Kundera, *The Art of the Novel* and *Testaments Betrayed*, is the problem of the crisis experienced by a drifting society, by a world contemplating its crash. Kundera believes that the crisis is noticeable in "the monster" coming from outside: *History*; it is the obsessive history present in the works of Musil, Broch, or Kafka. The reasons progress in the writer's essays: only because the novel is able to depict, thanks to the novelist's complicity, the events of a threatening and tragic ending (see Kundera, 2000, p. 11). The novelist (and not the writer!, as Kundera warns us) and *the novel's intelligence* represent the terms of the equation interpreted as poles of the narrative work formed through its own intelligence included in the intimate, organic substance of the literary work. In its century-long meditation, the novel enquires about human existence. It is not impossible for "the novel's intelligence", decided not by the writer's brutal intervention but by the *inner forces* of the narrative text, to be explained also by way of the rediscovery – in the readings and performances of the end of the XX century – of the XVIII century novel (Laurence Sterne, Fielding, Diderot, Richardson and Goethe), where the narrative composition (accidental), the discourse, the digression, the ellipse, the fragmentation and the heterogeneity of the verbal discourses metamorphose the forms. Musil, Broch, Gombrowicz, and before them Kafka and Joyce, broke the rules and the literary canon, creating a freer perspective, more direct and less subjected to the crystallized poetics (including the analysis of the XX century novel).

Actually, *the novel becomes the text, namely, a world of signs*, building a semiotics of the genre's signs, not in conformity with the reader's habits. A heteroclite universe is born in the novel by inserting humor and grotesque, thus giving the genre a freedom unimaginable before. This is evident in the Latin-American prose (Borges, Cortázar, Bioy Casares, Márques in the postures of story-teller and reporter), in the Italian prose (Italo Calvino, Pier Paolo Pasolini), and in one of the most fascinating books of the Russian prose: the novel of Andrei Bitov, *Pushkin House*. The always mentioned heterogeneity, the carnivalesque sounds and the bitter humor increase through the book's obvious intertextuality. The intertextual references are so numerous that they are actually part of an intelligent and reflexive game. The intertextuality is created by means of numerous references, comments on the text, and by imagining an inciting meta-text, having a surprising depth of ideas, a depth conjugated with elements absorbed in the narrative discourse. Certainly, the XX century prose takes other pathways as well, some amplified by the contact with the experience initiated by Kafka; the absurd and the overbidding of the game of the irrational and of the illogic; the suppression of the narrative's traditional formulas welcomes us through the prose of the absurd, the prose of the deconstruction of the real and the breaking of those limits accepted so far in the evolution of the novel following Kafka, Joyce, Musil or Broch: a new narrative "intelligence" radicalizes the vision and stirs up inside the narrative forms; this is the case of Witold Gombrowicz, one of the most interesting figures of the novel created as anti-novel, as refusal to conform to tradition, to the truisms and the ordinary affirmations of a certain type of world representation. The *non-mimetic novel* is related thus to the narrative of Musil and Broch, to the novelists descending from this extraordinary experience of the XX century prose.

Milan Kundera rightly asserted that at the end of the XX century we were witnessing a re-examination and, probably more accurately said, a rehabilitation of the *narrative game*. The more open to innovative ways the game is, the more numerous and more eloquently formulated the rules are (cf. Milan Kundera, *Les Testaments trahis*, Gallimard, 1993).

The narrative's development is often surprising given the re-invention of certain archetypal models or the recreation of several canonical forms of the genre. The reading of *The Man without Qualities*, or of *The Sleepwalkers* (even more evident with regard to the co-played techniques), forces the re-evaluation of all the novel's criteria and coordinates. A new paradigm is thus established: it professes the narrative poly-voices and polyphony, the convergence and interference of various discourse types: the essay, the reflexive commentary, the verse, the song, and the dissertations (essaystically) focusing on several existential motifs etc. Therefore, it becomes natural for the proclamation of the essay's right to exist within the novel (see the XVIII century novel and its relations with the prose of the moralists, a prose of aphorisms and maxims broadened to short fable-narrations) to remove other restrictions, while establishing the digression, the rejection of the biography-characters, and above all while abandoning the characters with a psychological profile. The *game* becomes the key factor and its "emergence" allows the novel to revitalize its structures.

The novel's polyvalences exclude from the very beginning false and inoperable hierarchies within the order of the preferences for certain motifs, themes, narrative archetypes, character categories etc. The game associated with the humor, the grotesque, the comical or, synthetically, with the carnivalesque does not represent but one of the novel's dimensions, a genre with an infinitely larger and more open vocation. The sacred text, the myth, and the human manifestations within the genre of the sacred metamorphose within the novel in the manifestations of the profane (Kundera writes in *Testaments Betrayed*: "religion and humor are incompatible", in Kundera, 1993). However, the parody and the vision liberated from conventions and prejudices do not exclude the reinterpretation of the sacred or mythical text (see Thomas Mann's novel *Joseph and His Brothers*, or the recreation of the biblical story in William Faulkner's novel). The writer is often tempted to explain without betraying the nature of the narrative communication; this is what Thomas Mann does in "How I wrote Doctor Faustus"; the same novelist creates true dissertations on the themes capable of suggesting reading codes. Here is for example a fragment from *Joseph and His Brothers*, where the narrator unties the temporal mechanism of the book: "Because although we took over the unchanged sidereal mathematic time, of then and there, that is of days much preceding the wanders of the Ur man, and we will likewise transmit them even to the most distant descendents, nevertheless, the significance, the density and the plenitude of the earthly time are not identical everywhere and forever; time has an unequal measurement, even despite the caldean objectivity of our measurement of time; six centuries did not mean then, and under that sky, what they mean in our western history; that time was milder, more quiet, more balanced; time was less lively back then, the changing action of its uninterrupted work on things and on the world was more unhurried and meek – although during these twenty generations there had been important changes and revolutions, even *natural* transformations, within the close circle in which Joseph lived, transformations of the Earth's crust, the way we know about them and he knew about them as well. Where was, during his time, Gomorra, and where was Sodom, where Lot of Harran had settled, where were the fortresses of voluptuousness? There where its depravity had once flourished, the Dead Sea extended its lye waters, of lead, as a consequence of a country's collapse under a flood of fire, pitch and brimstone, so frightening and apparently so damaging that the daughters of Lot, who saved themselves together with their father – the same daughters he had wanted to give to the Sodoms to satisfy their cravings instead of some all too virtuous guests – thinking that there wasn't anyone else left alive on earth, seized by the female worry of keeping mankind alive, copulated with their father." (Th. Mann, *Iosif şi fraţii săi*, I, Bucharest, Univers, 1977).

The narrator's comments have multiple functions (here as auctorial narrator) - of "interpreter" and "chronicler" destined to re-create the myths and stories of the Old Testament. To some extent, Umberto Eco's observation on the text is valid: "each text is a lazy machine that requires the reader to do part of its work" (Umberto Eco, 1997). However, the participation of the receiver, the reader willing to re-read the literary work, is connected to the requests of a narrative creation always obsessed with the human destiny, with its existence. Therefore, the narrator's *meditation*, and the predisposition to reflection and to the meanings' elucidation belong to the modern novel's condition of being. Dostoevsky's notes for the *Demons*; the dissociations of the motifs and the crystallization of the themes, of the characters and of the plot become the compositional effort; the novel is, by excellence, construction, elaboration, architectural effort. Thus, the active conscience of the novelists belonging to the family of Joyce, Lowry, Musil, Broch, Thomas Mann, determined to place the novel's structural invariants on the level of ideas and reflexivity. If Musil's narrative is a creation of the thought and of the intellectual height (the novel is the product of a dramatic and laborious analytic and interpretative process, a rational process always presided by the novelist's perspective, untroubled by details), no novel can "dissolve" in a treaty or a philosophical essay. It is an artistic reality; its intellectuality comes from observation and from the scrutinizing outlook on time, human beings and their universe. The narrative creation privileges the individual subjected to anamneses and examined within the unmistakable space of the epic.

In the end, it depends on the readers and on the quality of their readings, on the formation and the "library" indissolubly connected to their spiritual biography because, it needs to be known, the novel exists, I have said it before, in the self-telic reality, as a cosmic universe called to speak to the people. The universes of the XX century novel are worlds where the characters face extraordinary adventures, experiences of the spirit, of History; they face anxieties impossible to dissipate or to weaken, they discover in their surroundings a humanity emerged from a true vanity fair; the readers begin to understand one of the conditions of this creation: the return and reinterpretation of the works that have never been totally revealed or consumed with regard to meanings, resonances and projections in a time that is to come eventually. I think it is appropriate to mention here one of the most suggestive reflections of Lucian Blaga from *Pietre pentru templul meu* ("Stones for my temple"): "Those who dealt with the history of the problems men had thought about could notice that «the mysterious», «the enigmatic» which we remove from a question, from anything – appears somewhere else. The more we explain mysteries with the help of a phenomenon or a law, the more enigmatic they become: thus, I could happily refer to a «*principle of the conservation of the enigmas*»" (Author's emphasis, L. Blaga, *Opere*, volume 7, "Eseuri", Bucharest, Minerva, 1980).

***

Svidrigad'lov from Dostoevsky's *Crime and Punishment* is a bizarre and extremely complex character, expression of disconcerting features. A combination of demoniac features, but also a human being with strange attributes, a mixture of evil and often-opposing-evil impulses, Svidrigad'lov is a keen reader. In the loneliness of the countryside mansion, Svidrigad'lov meditates about the world. His numerous readings recall the motifs represented in contemporary literature, but especially in Dostoevskyian prose. Amoral, a seducer haunted by crimes and pedophilia, leaving in his shadow hunches of abominable actions, Svidrigad'lov is confusing due to his good deeds situated at the opposing pole of his inclinations. There is in Svidrigad'lov a tragic, demoniac inner disorder which determines him to finally commit suicide.

During one of his conversations with Raskolnikov, a complex and ambiguous character (cf. Valeriu Cristea, *Dicţionarul personajelor lui Dostoievski*, Bucharest, Cartea Românească, 1983), being worried and tortured by the unknown, he asks himself about "eternity": "«Men always represent eternity as an incomprehensible idea, as something immense - immense! But why should this necessarily be the case? Imagine, on the contrary, a small room – a bathroom if you will – blackened by smoke, with spiders in every corner. Supposing that to be eternity! I often conceive it to be so». «What! Do you mean to say that you have not a more just, a more consolidating idea of eternity?» exclaimed Raskolnikoff, ill at ease. «More just, you ask? Who knows? This point of view is possibly true, and certainly would be so if I had my way» answered Svidrigad'lov, with a vague smile. (Fyodor Dostoevsky, *Crime and punishment*, London, Penguin Popular Classics, 1997; p. 220).

Fyodor Dostoevsky obsessively monitored the great world's novelists till the end of their careers or their lives. The most expressive and overwhelming confessions are their creations; under the sign of the great Russian novelist's creations, literature reaffirmed its right to be and to examine - *differently* from all the other forms of human knowledge - the human existence of people with dramas and tragic experiences, and thus inviting the reader to meditate, merging rationality with emotions in a scholarly and unknown combination, over the world seen under the threat of History, not as science, but as the destiny of each individual projected in the great literature of the narrative.

Alternatives within the poetics of the novel

Richard Rorty's assertions on the novel, by and large inspired by the reflections of Milan Kundera collected in *The Art of the Novel*, are only partially well-founded; his inclination for polemics and generalizations forces a certain, not only theoretical, wariness. However, one of his comments is worth mentioning: there are genres "born as reactions and alternatives to the attempt to *theorize* the human problems" (Richard Rorty, *Pragmatism şi filosofie post-nietzscheană*. Eseuri filosofice, 2, Bucharest, Univers, 2000). The emphasis belongs to the author, passionate about Kundera's work and especially by the poetics formulated by the Czech writer.

The novel continues to rediscover its original sources and its spiritual essences. I label them as such because the novel solves the false dichotomy (philosophy – literature – fictional universe) in its own ways, including the *ascetic meditation* of the novelist determined to remain, through destiny and communication, *a story-teller, a creator of narrative histories*, of imaginary beings and of perfectly credible worlds as vast Utopias of existence. The abovementioned exegete writes that "we, philosophers, carry within us at least a tiny bit of an ascetic priest. We all yearn for essence and share the preference for theory as opposing the story-telling" (Rorty, 2000). The "ascetic priest" seems situated in irreconcilable opposition with the novelist (in our case); however, reality is infinitely more complex as regards the tectonic movements caused by the absolutely unpredictable, disconcerting even, history of narrative forms reborn from original models, recreated and forced to interpret on the stage of human history a performance overwhelming as magnitude and depth, as scenery for the mankind's development which is continuously threatened by the existential tragic, by the prophetic voices of these "prophet-story-tellers".

The reality is that the lights of philosophy do not overstep, if I might refer to it as such, the sacred, already acknowledged territories of the novel; Nietzsche's revelation of tragic knowledge, of the adventure of the individuals crushed by their destiny, also belongs to the novelist obsessed, from the epic histories' beginnings onwards, by the phases of an ontology over which the specter of the tragic and the warnings of an undeniable *Apocalypse*, projected in the vision of a humanity suffering from loneliness and indecipherable existential problems, are constant themes. Despite the epic formula and the dominant features of the great creations, the experience and the alternatives of the novel are essentially infinite. The temptations, I say it again, of generalizing and annulling other mechanisms of knowledge (philosophy versus literature and, especially, versus novel) are frequent; there is no reason for the rational and also appropriate exam of the narrative forms to be bothered by them. R.-M. Albérès turned the balance to the resources of literature by believing, restrictively and unconvincingly, that literature has higher chances in its investigations into lived life – the existential tragic (cf. R.-M. Albérès *L'aventure intelectuelle du XX-e siècle*, 4th edition, Albin Michel, 1969). By generalizing, the French researcher, or better said the French literary historian, sometimes attracted by literary categories, presents "the literary sensibility" (?) as "barometer" (the only one!) for the premonitory vocation of literature and for interpreting the present ("Those who write a novel «sense» the time of tomorrow, the moral or immoral wind that will blow, the storm of History [...]." (R.-M. Albérès, 1969, p. 9).

Such "meteorology" (a metaphorism of incontestable intellectual insufficiency) cannot impose a balanced and rational judgment on the novel's adventure, a work of ample vision and passionate affirmation of the Narrative as an essential mechanism of knowledge. In reality, the novel continues to be, beyond the extremely agitated and complicated diagram of its forms' evolution, a human experience, an experience of human loneliness surrounded by anxieties and uncertainties, by inner fears and degraded, often gravely interrupted inter-human relations. Both literature and philosophy have often revealed the individual's loneliness and his absolute impossibility to communicate (cf. Claude-Edmond Magny, *Littérature et critique*, Payot, 1971; p. 193). The retrospective advanced in this well-articulated volume is interesting as great part of the 1900s-1930s literature is set under the mark of the *expressionism* seen as a solution for the interpreters of those processes and phenomena intensely felt in an epic manner: Hauptmann, Heinrich Mann, Franz Werfel and, by extrapolating, also Virginia Woolf or Proust, John Dos Passos and Alfred Döblin would have realized, at least partly, the expressionist aesthetic of profound and dramatic contrasts, torturing destiny developments etc. I find more significant the inclusion in this group of James Joyce and his narrative. The characteristics of the Irish writer's novel equally represent the attributes of certain fundamental works of the European narrative and mainly of Kafka's creations.

"We live in a universe where nothing, and under no circumstances, happens to give the illusion of reality; [...] the hope of some outburst is just deception. The individual, willingly or not, is caught in an undefined system of causes, known or unknown to him" (C.-E. Magny, 1971, p. 303). A veritable aggression on time ("*mettre à nu sa foncière imposture*"), the unraveling and the degradation of time are actually the object of a prose charged with an intellectual tension that forces us to return to the XVIII century novel, to the essay and to the digressive discourse of many famous thinkers.

***

The poetics and the theory of the narrative in general, at least in Romania, still have to revisit and rediscover the coordinate of the *novel-essay* and of the "intellectual" novel; namely, the novelist captured by the idea and captivated by the resources of a *philosophical account* (an alternative to the strictly eventful novel, the "history" novel, the novel endowing with multiple implications the plot, narrative strategies, the characters' organization and placement in various situations – regardless of the characters' nature and adopted solutions –, the novel of strong and irreducible conflicts etc.) chooses the options where the narrator and the resources of narrative story do not smother or destroy the works' reflexive network.

Supporter of the novel sustained by the idea's pathos (the philosophical novel), Milan Kundera does not ignore the properties by no means uniformed and lacking substance of the novel seen as work of narrative developments, of the fascinating epic event imagined by the narrator: "The way Nietzsche (I anticipate by saying that for both Robert Musil and Hermann Broch the German philosopher is the emblematic personality constantly evoked) brought philosophy closer to the novel, likewise Musil brought the novel closer to philosophy. And it is not a matter of Musil being less of a novelist or Nietzsche less of a philosopher" (Milan Kundera, *Les Testaments trahis*, Gallimard, 1993; p. 208). The readings suggested in these essays are not intended in any way to ignore or betray the specificity of the discourse and of the novel's acknowledged properties. Its forms continue to capture us trough the created universes, through the spaces of narrative fictions and, naturally, through the epic adventure of some destinies, regardless of whether they are just symbols as Joseph K. or the topographer who arrived in the vicinity of the Castle, or ample representations like in a vast chronicle-novel, a *Bildungsroman*, a tetralogy such as *Joseph and His Brothers* (a memorable reflection about time and about its duration removed from "history"), or in an ample and unfinished masterpiece like *The Man without Qualities* or the three perspective-characters of the narrative Time in *The Sleepwalkers*.

Thus, reiterating Kundera's statements from *Testaments Betrayed*, the novel maintains its own poetics which it develops and opens to the idea, and its own constituents, beyond numerous evolutions and beyond the tensions of the "great" History which should not be ignored or eluded.

The novels published after 1900, especially those following

World War I (I do not intend to make time divisions or determine certain features generated by the decades prior to the Second World War!), discover a phenomenon having extremely broad implications for the history of the form: (mainly) through Joyce and the writers in Europe rummaged by the First World War, a new continent of the genre is explored: that of the *post-psychologizing* novel; the solutions, the mechanics, the routine, the exhaustion and the devitalized variants of the Proustian novel lose their authority without letting the phenomenon eliminate the psychoanalysis's echoes and solutions, while Freud was still being followed and acclaimed. It is true that the narrators' attitude and the options are different; instead of the dilemmatic character, of the introspection and the *leitmotivs* (oscillations, continuous interrogations, obsession, subconscious etc.), there is a more subtle and raw revelation of the human being. The topographer in Franz Kafka's novel is assisted in all his attempts, paralyzed and gradually subjected to an inexorable degradation; Hans Castorp experiments and discovers a world of ideas ignored until then, without however finding salvation; Felix Krull has the revelation of illusion, of appearances and of a brutal reality (the actor Müller-Rosé, fascinating on stage and revolting without his make-up; Thomas Mann, *The Confessions of Felix Krull*); Pasenow, Esch and Huguenau, the characters in *The Sleepwalkers*, are projected on the background of a shaken Germany, fatally destined to an inevitable and implacable destruction.

***

I believe that the novel reader is a special category, an implicit reader and an always engaged reader (Wolfgang Iser, *The Fictive and the Imaginary*, The John Hopkins University Press, 1993), the reader carries the memory of the creations; the reader remakes the course and the unpredictable movement of the destinies, finding nonetheless, according to a privileged "fatality", the fundamental creations, *the models*: Rabelais and Cervantes, Grimmelshausen, the XVIII century English and French novels, the gothic novel etc.; the lines of the form's evolution are constantly recalled; the creations are re-lived thanks to this reader equipped for multiple references and for an exercise of intertextual memory; the processes are absolutely necessary; they inflict a new life on the books. The "traveling" reading chosen by Thomas Mann is *Don Quixote*; like in a reading log, the author of *The Magic Mountain* notes: "Yesterday afternoon and evening I read some pages from *Don Quixote*, accompanied by the music from the blue salon. I want to continue the reading, tucked in an armchair on the deck, which represents a transposition to the other extreme of the excellent chaise-long of Hans Castorp" (*Călătorie pe mare cu Don Quijote*, in *Patimirile şi măreţia maeştrilor*, Editura Muzicală a Uniunii Compozitorilor, 1972). I think there is another interesting observation made by Mann, the author who has the merit of having drawn attention to the works of Robert Musil; furthermore, according to a late exegesis, he was the first to define the fundamental book of Musil, *The Man without Qualities*, as the expression of a supreme *intellectuality*. The quality described as such – we know it very well now – equals rational vision, a comprehensive examination of the causal factors and the tragic depiction of the world in its irreversible downfall.

I would also like to add that Thomas Mann, after rereading Cervantes, detects the nature of "the epic humor", the comic of a certain structure and substance (a "*pathetic comic*", notes the reader-traveler), associating to his vision from *Joseph and His Brothers* the extraordinary adventures of Simplicius Simplicissimus, a true archetype in German literature and the forerunner of Goethe's great creations. Essentially, one of the most productive directions of the European narrative initiated and opened by Kafka is that of the *tragic-comic*, of the *absurd grotesque*, of the rational and of the irrationality's aggression. And over everything watches the eternal look of a form where the heterogeneity and the variable development shape both the *meditation-novel* and the essential ontological *experience-novel*. Therefore, the "ascetic priests", the philosophers who are more or less convinced by the functions of the narrative, are obliged to relive their own observations about the human condition through the novel and its energies.

We are always accompanied by the trip taken by Leopold Bloom through the Dublin of Stephen Dedalus: "the publicity agent" is the tragic witness of an immense parody similar to that of Gogol or Kafka, a parody highly developed in the unfinished work of Robert Musil. It is not a wonder that Hermann Broch was also an admirer of Joyce and that the great Latin-American writers, Jorge Luis Borges, Bioy Casares, Julio Cortázar, Gabriel Garcia Márquez, referred on various occasions to that *something else* initiated, proclaimed and accomplished by Kafka and his followers. The novelist Witold Gombrowicz too has to be included in this list. If *Ulysses* programmatically professes the referential network of the world's spiritual and cultural Memory, *The Man without Qualities* absorbs them within the very heteroclite formula of the discourse, like Broch, where the essayist digression, the songs and the "traditional" narrative (relativized) levels conjugate under the sign of the diversity and plurality of voices.

In *Doctor Faustus*, whose subtitle reminds us of the formula used in the XVIII century novel – "The Life of the German Composer Adrian Leverkühn, As Told by a Friend" –, the counterpoint discourse, the alternations and the interruption of the narrative rhythm through the insertion of the narrator's voice (Serenus Zeitblom) engage us in a history of demonology and of the myths of a world tragically made to feel guilty. The epic extension is extraordinary and the combining elements compel us to place the novel within the lineage of Goethe and of the later experiences of the German expressionist school; when talking about Adrian, the chronicler-narrator relives (the "biography" is written, within a different type of conventions, in 1944 – a tragic moment for the German people) manifestations of the main character: "Not without my acknowledging", records Serenus, "that the *tragedy* and the *comedy* grew on the same trunk and it was enough to change the light just a little bit, to pass from one to the other." (Th. Mann, *Doctor Faustus*, Bucharest, E.L.U., 1966).

There is an inimitable and distinctive regime of the narrative and of the stated views; the chronicler cannot avoid some considerations about history. They are symptomatic for the type of novel written in this space, where the myths of the creator, the performance of a demonology salvaged by creations belong, in a final analysis, to a tragic history. The same phenomena are recognizable in the narrative creations of Broch and Musil, in the novel of Elias Canetti or the allegories of Hermann Hesse. Their followers of the Second World War generation would not write differently: Günter Grass or Heinrich Böll, writers obsessed with the experience of their forerunners, with the appeal to their fundamental model, Franz Kafka. Returning to the "narrator" in *Doctor Faustus, obsessed by this double chronology*, that is "the time of the narrator and the time of the narration", for a third projection to be possible, "considered by the reader suitable to receive my account"; in other words, *a triple chronology* re-dimensions the work, the general and configurative vision, crushed by the tragic nature of the events: the inevitable downfall of Nazi Germany.

Therefore, it should be mentioned that there is a generous and at the same time tragic juxtaposition of events, having a time movement shaped by the memory of the narrators and by their meditation, the higher evidence of epic development. The novel by Thomas Mann dates from 1947 and the diary of the novel was written in 1949 ("How I wrote «Doctor Faustus»"). It is an exemplary *poetics* representative for the writing of Thomas Mann and his contemporaries or followers. Protean and heterogeneous, the narration appeals often to *parody*, under the impulse of lucidity and rationality. Thomas Mann confesses: "As to the style, I know nothing but parody. In this regard I am close to Joyce." (Th. Mann, "Cum am scris «Doctor Faustus»", 1949, in *Doctor Faustus*, E.P.L.U., 1966). The transposition into fiction of several serious Historic issues creates, not only in the abovementioned novel, a narrative formula where reality and imagination, experiencing multiple anamorphous processes, realize a world in the face of which it is impossible to remain indifferent, beyond the deviations from the traditional model of the novel's narration.

The chronicler in *Doctor Faustus* matured in the spirit of the rigor and ethics announced in the German space by Martin Luther. His somber and at the same time trenchant discourse, the discipline of the thought and the guarded rhetoric of the argumentation (cf. Martin Luther, *Scrieri*, vol. I, Logos, 2003) have created for German spirituality, throughout its tormented history, a fervor and a rationalism permanently tempted to critically question any statement. Luther's meditation has generated a scholarly direction of German philosophy or Lichtenberg's skeptical meditation and polemic. The "emancipation" unleashed by Luther in the XV-XVI centuries is to be found in German literature without being totally challenged by the experiences of the XX century prose. One of Mann's statements ratifies the opinions mentioned above: "It is necessary, when you yourself are present in front of a serious narration, *to keep contact with the great epic creations...*" (Th. Mann, 1966). It would be now possible to revisit, by just remembering them, his short-stories because they have the value of "poetics" open to the aesthetic conscience of German literature and, generally, to the paramount themes of the XX century novel. If the revelation of beauty and the feeling of failure (*Death in Venice*) are the occasion for tormented deliberations projected through the effect of narrative self-referentiality, in *Tonio Kröger* we discover a discourse essential for the act of creation and for the myth of the artist determined to sacrifice himself/herself for his/her art: "He worked in silence, in invisible privacy, for he utterly despised those minor hacks who treated their talents as a social ornament – who, whether they were poor or rich, whether they affected an unkempt and shabby appearance or sumptuous individualistic neckwear, aimed above all else at living happily, charmingly and artistically, little suspecting that good work is brought forth only under the pressure of a bad life, that living and working are incompatible and that *one must have died if one is to be wholly a creator*." (My emphasis added, Thomas Mann, *Tonio Kröger*, in "Death in Venice and Other Stories", Vintage Classics, 1998, p. 155).

Like in a myth of eternal return, the creator follows certain principles; an *ethos* presides over the burnings of the creator and his sacrifice.

***

The novelists analyzed in these pages are often brutal and ruthless with their characters; Pasenow and Huguenau in *The Sleepwalkers* by Broch; Ulrich in *The Man without Qualities* are not the victims of their environment and time; frequently sanctioned, analyzed without any kindness, rejected by the other "actors" of the universe imagined by the novelists, the heroes belong to a fictional reality ongoing full disintegration. Useless or cowards, accepting the compromises, they represent the ending of an era. *"The hermetic story"* in *The Magic Mountain* is actually cleared up because it announced the beginning of a gradual and fatal degradation. "This celebration of death" will start soon and it is difficult to grasp what will follow this carnage unleashed for a seriously ill mankind... (cf. *Muntele vrăjit*, Bucharest, E.L.U., 1967).

Between the reflections of Settembrini and the wise lines of Naphta, the somber and dark image of the ending is interpreted as the end of a world and of an empire ("[...] in the rotted empire whose capital is [Vienna], the mummy of the Sacred Roman Empire of German nation!", Ibid.), reason of the vast and ambitious meditation of Musil in *The Man without Qualities.*

"[...] And he tried to demonstrate to me that music could begin by being a word, that it could be created and prepared through words" (*Doctor Faustus*). The reflections of Adrian Leverkühn detect the nature of the Logos, an epiphany of the creation subordinated to thinking. The composer's works (the symbolic representation of the Creator formed in Germany's tragic space), *Apocalipsis cum figures* and the cantata *The Lamentation of Doctor Faustus* embody, through the languages' syncretic conjugation, an appeal to rationality and, at the same time, they announce the ending and the mystery of the downfall. This is the central theme of the abovementioned works, indissolubly and organically connected to the creations of Kafka and Joyce. They do not only generate the model but they also illustrate the magical force of the warnings transmitted thanks to a multitude of forms, languages, stances of the individual involved in the ending's hallucinating agitation.

An original treaty of demonology can be put together from

the works of these great novelists tortured by questions, on a quest for always delayed answers. The great personalities of the end of the XIX century, philosophers or artists like Nietzsche and Wagner; the symbolist and post-symbolist poetry; *expressionism* (Stefan George, Georg Trakl, Rainer Maria Rilke); the prose of Arthur Schnitzler, open to inner monologue and to a character outlined through the insistence of self-referentiality etc.; the spiritual effervescence of Vienna (I will revisit this phenomenon analyzed from a totally surprising perspective given the connections revealed in the admirable book by Ion Vartic, *Cioran naiv şi sentimental*, "Biblioteca Apostrof", 2000); the emergence of innovative ideas; the spirit of an avant-garde perfectly controlled by Idea represents the fertile territory of the literature of Musil, Broch and, before them, the literature of Thomas Mann, the most authorized voice for stating *the themes of the Apocalypse* purified and examined by analysts with multiple and labyrinthical instruments of investigation in the decades following World War II.

A world was created through suffering and the confrontation of ideas; passions and devouring fervors have prepared the literature of the novelists named above. *Like in Adrian Leverkühn's tragic history filled with warnings, the forerunners signed the pact with the devil and suffered for their creation.* Thomas Mann wrote an unforgettable page for the 50th anniversary of the death of Richard Wagner. It could serve as an emblematic statement for understanding the culture torn by deep convulsions and anxieties: "The art of Richard Wagner was the great passion, the great love of Nietzsche. He loved it the same way Baudelaire loved it, the poet of the *Fleurs du Mal*, about whom one can say that even in agony, paralysis and during the partial idiotization of his last days he smiled joyfully when Wagner's name was quoted – *il a souri d'allegrèsse.* / In the same way, during his paralytic night, Nietzsche quivered when he heard this name and answered: «I loved him so much»" (Th. Mann, *Măreţia şi patimile lui Richard Wagner*, in "Patimirile şi măestria maeştrilor").

This is a state of mind captivating for many creators and philosophers who, after years of History's draconic lessons and after severe deviations from the brutally and bloodily broken moral laws, returned later on to examine culture's value and meaning (unaltered by the events). And Thomas Mann is one of those few artists in German literature (more precisely, an artist of German expression, to include thus the artists from the other countries of the pre- and post-war political geography) whose active and non-indulgent conscience drew attention on a great literature dominated by Idea and by the supreme rationality of the intelligence shaped at the school of ideas. I already said that the works of Musil, unfinished and projected on extremely broad dimensions, found in Thomas Mann one of the most enthusiast readers and, implicitly, commentators too. He used to refer to the *intellectuality* (to be read: intellectual depth) of the novel *The Man without Qualities* - history and epic meditation about the world in the vision and evolution of a true interpreter and analyst. It is not surprising that an admirer of the two German authors, Milan Kundera, will give a relatively identical characterization. Kundera writes in *Testaments Betrayed*: "Both of them are novelists of massive intellectual ability" (Kundera, 1993). As regards Musil, the domination of the idea and of the reflexive discourse is consistently maintained in the general tonality of the chapters and, equally, in the short-stories, notes and barely drafted projects. Thus, it suggests a certain manner of reading and, moreover, a certain manner of *re-reading*; because, beyond any other considerations (Ion Ianoşi wrote numerous intelligent comments in the preface and the postscript of the Romanian edition of *The Man without Qualities*), Musil's work builds up; it is the privilege of narrative fictions, an essential universe, generalizing and generalized/conceptualized *only* through the instruments of epic creation, imagining a quintessence-character for an unforgettable history.

According to R.M. Albérès, the fundamental significance of Musil's work would be the *search* for the phenomena/phenomenon that gives finality to human existence. Quoting Max Scheler (neither the scientific anthropology, nor the philosophic or the strictly theoretical anthropologies generate a unitary and coherent vision on the individual), the French essayist bestows on the novel the right to meditate on mankind from a global and universal standpoint. The work's creative principle is defined by the cognitive pathos of Musil's work, by the acceptance of a *total "examination"*, by the setting in motion of all the fields of human knowledge and their materialization in the structures characteristic to the narrative form.

There is perfect agreement, as regards these statements, with Kundera's passionate and highly admiring reading. The narrative of Musil and Broch communicate a "distinct, concrete metaphysics". The end or the twilight of the psychological/psychologizing novel can also be explained by the taking on a goal abandoned or neglected by philosophy: the knowledge of existence, of the human life seen in its individuality and existential pathways.

The fact that Heidegger (see Richard Rorty, 2000) ignored the novel, made him neglect an inexhaustible territory of confessions about the human being, thus diminishing the value of his opinions (cf. Milan Kundera, 1993). It is not a matter of changing or switching the roles in the broad performance of knowledge, and it is even less a matter of hierarchies, completely accomplished in literary theory. The "collaboration" of anthropology and philosophy with... the novel denotes essentially the assimilation or absorption within the novel of the pathways opened and covered by humanity's thinking, often tempted by metaphysics and less by the zones where the individual reveals his/her essences, his/her identity and concrete, alive breath. How is it possible that a British writer, born after World War II, in his meditation on History and on the humanity imprisoned by these codes of History remains so close to the novelists who were besmirched in the trenches of World War I (Ernst Jünger, Roland Dorgélès, Ernest Hemingway, Erich Maria Remarque or in Romania, Liviu Rebreanu, Felix Aderca, Cezar Petrescu, Gib I. Mihăescu, Victor Ion Popa etc.), and later were terrified by the warnings of a second conflagration which, in most cases, they ended up experiencing in exile? The explanation lies in the same persistent and unyielding return to the story; to be more precise, to the history-story, creating the Utopia of a world attracted by the Apocalypse.

The Brit Graham Swift, admiring Dickens (symptomatic for the forms' poetics!), imagines the drama of a history teacher at a London college, who experienced the war, the traumas of the German bombings, a conflict that mutilated his life; hour after hour, he puts together a non-exemplary Histrionics-History, allowing people to forget: their amnesias – far from rescuing them ("Every so often, there are these attempts to jettison the impedimenta of history", Graham Swift, *Waterland*, London, Picador, 1999; p. 136). However, the teacher of historic utopias ponders: "There are no compasses for journeying in time." (Swift, 1999, p. 135). One of the chapters of Swift's "Faulkner-like" novel (the antagonist history of certain families, with their tragic heritage and the "leaving" of time through sacrifices) is entitled "De la Révolution", typical of Montaigne's essays, but the questions and the examples are the components of a "history" more likely related to Scheherazade, to the temptation of that invariable and always fascinating "Once upon a time": "How is it that every so often history demands a bloodbath, a Holocaust, an Armageddon? And why is it that every time the time before has taught us nothing?" (Ibid., p. 141).

The Man without Qualities remained an incomplete work and it could be argued that such a project of great proportions would have been difficult to have been entirely realized. As memoirist, Elias Canetti spoke about the unique nature of Musil's novel; the author of the *Auto-da-Fe* noted that the writer could not have guessed that his work "had been conceived for a twofold eternity: not only for immortality, but also for incompletion" (Elias Canetti, *Jocul privirilor*, Bucharest, Dacia, 1989). An acute sensibility and an insight absorbed by the total "rationalization" and conceptualization of impressions, memory, information etc. make Musil an *interpreter*, a spirit of everlasting internal combustion, refusing nonetheless, most definitely, the Freudian-type analysis excluded from the series of possible models; as compared to Hermann Broch, a Freudian by absolute adhesion, but less influenced by the suggestions of psychoanalysis. The characters, their relations, the nature and their reasons originate in a different direction: *the lucid observation* and - the affirmation needs to be understood as perfect detachment and objectification – *the scientific observation*; it is rather an exam based on the study of social-human etiology and on a network of information used in the anamnesis produced just like in a medical file accompanied by the cold numbers of laboratory investigations.

Like Thomas Mann, the author of *The Man without Qualities* comes from the tradition of German medieval prose, from the fervent and fanatic Lutheran discourse or from the narrative of Grimmelshausen. Between the passionate and still reserved demonstration of Erasmus of Rotterdam and the addresses of the man who would speak up new principles at the University of Wittenberg, the lesson of truth and gravity is kept as a model by Musil. Furthermore, the German writer reveals his affinities and readings in his novel. The phenomenon of analysis and severe study of the psycho-sociological symptoms of their human "geography" is of course a common place, known in the world's literatures. The prose of Faulkner is obsessed, in the first part of the cycle Yoknapatawpha, by the traumas and the consequences of World War I, without later ignoring the bad omens of the 1930s and 1940s. More insistent and in a true paroxysmal tension, the narrator in Henry Miller's trilogy "The Rosy Crucifixion" will fix tragic accents when he comments on the sick human environment following World War II. The feeling of an eternal threat, of the world crashed and overwhelmed by the alternatives of extinction is converted in a representation mined with convulsions like in an apocalypse without any chances of salvation (cf. Henry Miller, *Plexus*, Buchet-Chastel). Undoubtedly, the continuous appeal to the magic of Dostoevsky's universe, apparent in the creations of all the great writers of the XX century, has a constant echo in Musil's work. Thus, the knowledge of and the belief in the lucid and ruthless experience, but also the attraction for a huge diversity of forms, characters, solutions; thus, the nature of the discourse, sometimes ironical and tempted by parody, sometimes grave or even pathetic, other times accusing and uptight. The world risks its survival, willing to deceive itself or to prolong the deceiving unconsciousness of its forerunners.

Canetti, a witness of the Viennese period of Musil's and Broch's lives (Musil's antipathy for the author of *The Sleepwalkers* had been provoked by the impression that Broch's trilogy drew more than a lot on the already published parts of *The Man without Qualities*) rightly observed with revelatory nuances for the discourse professed in the novel: "For him [Musil] everything arose from something accurate and aspired to something accurate" (Canetti, 1989); thus, this explains why Musil did not accept Joyce for what the German author called the "atomization" of language. Nevertheless, attracted by the *Gestalt* psychology, he produces narrative structures sustained by a system of invariants capable of giving an impulse to form, of structuring through the form's rigor. This is the reason for which the novel is organized on a network of motifs focused on several fundamental themes: the shameful failure of the intellectual; Kakania and its parody of an end, unwoven and metamorphosed in a pitiful parody; the hierarchy of the empire at its historic end; the human relations and their degrading – a true phenomenology of this empire grown old and totally stiff.

***

The novel of a decomposing world, *The Man without Qualities*, was written between 1921 and 1942 (the first volume was published in 1930 in Hamburg and the second in 1933, accompanied by an editorial note - "The first part of the second volume"; and finally, the first posthumous edition, known as the Frisé edition, was published in 1952. The fate of this book was not all that unruffled; the translators of the English edition, Robert Kaiser and Eithne Wilkins, produced a radically different hypothesis about the organization and order of the "file", concerning the parts left unfinished by the writer who had died in 1942. In 1978 Frisé advanced an exceptional structure given the accomplished effort and workload. Consequently, the first two parts or "books" are followed by the first 38 chapters of the third book (published during the author's life), and as regards the remains: the chapters 39-128 and "other posthumous fragments" were more logically and appropriately organized; these are simple files and quasi-completed "chapters"; sketches for projected chapters etc. The whole is truly impressive.

The German literary historian Fritz Martini considers "The gigantic and still fragmentary novel" a creation of "high philosophical and psychological intellectuality". Or, considering the themes' genre: "the sharpest analysis of the times' spirit"; "a subtle, profound work, full of ironical-melancholic depth" (Fritz Martini, *Istoria literaturii germane de la începuturi până în prezent*, Bucharest, Univers, 1972). I would like to emphasize the fact that the short considerations of the aforementioned literary historian are nothing but statements ratified in the numerous and extremely fertile interpretations of many researchers of the XX century novel.

A potential *anatomy of the work* should begin by reiterating Thomas Mann's defense of the novel. Following the publishing of the first volume (1920-21), a moment with no echoes or significant critical comments, the author of *The Magic Mountain* launched a first invitation for its reading by emphasizing, as already noted above, the book's intellectual height; some time later, when he was at Princeton, Mann referred to the oeuvre's value (cf. Jean-Pierre Maurel, "Présentation" to *L'homme sans qualités*, tome l'Éditions du Seuil, 1995). I believe that the dominant features of *The Man without Qualities* are to be found in the depth of the socio-philosophic vision on human condition, as well as in the minute and spectral analysis of a mutilating empire, mutilated by conservationism and immobility, by hierarchical imbecility, an empire somewhat connected to the tsarist empire through the schizophrenia of hierarchy, of casts, and of the crashing of the deformed and suppressed personality. A "*cheerful apocalypse*" contemplates its destructive factors, while admiring its "Committee of the Apocalypse". Jean-Pierre Maurel calls the optic of the novelist "*the despaired ferocity*" (Maurel, 1995, p. III) of a witness invited, through the absurd game of the events and of destiny, to watch the ending of a dying person. Any chance of healing is excluded from the very beginning; firstly, because the intellectuals are the main agent of a lucid and clinical research and hence, the presentation of the factors generating the ending. The cultural and artistic brilliancy, the great brotherhood of the Viennese spirit of late XIX century and early XX century produce, finally and not at all paradoxically, the "file" of a downfall: the court, the senile emperor surrounded by the sufficiency of the royal aristocracy; the ever more pronounced taste for the kitsch and the incompatible social and national contrasts shake the hybrid and heteroclite composition. Musil discovers an observer of all upheavals and decompositions: Ulrich, the diabolical agent of cruelty and of the cold, sterile, and therefore, tragic contemplation.

According to Cornel Ungureanu, these are the "circles" of the empire's geography, with its centre and peripheries, still so connected and "disconnected" with regard to human relations, identity and non- and anti-imperial nostalgias (Danilo Kiš, Witold Gombrowicz); each writer uses a different narrative collection of "instruments"; probably the most violent one given its derision and parody is the one used by Gombrowicz (see Cornel Ungureanu, *Mitteleuropa periferiilor*, Iaşi, Polirom, 2002). The literatures' common properties are contradicted, only partially, by the unmistakable experience and vision of Franz Kafka's work. That *something else* intensely felt by the succeeding writers (and not by the Czech writer's contemporaries) does not exclude the communication and observation of certain phenomena, symptoms and causes, immanent to this unsuccessful and flimsy construction of the two-headed imperial eagle.

There are elements able to determine and draw the specific and common lines of the two empires recreated also literarily: the imperial tsarist universe of Gogol or Chekhov (depicted in his sketches, short stories and accounts), of Tolstoy's and Dostoevsky's prose, not foreign to the absurd, the irrational, the violence and the alienation, connected to the world of Schnitzler, Martin Buber, Franz Werfel, Heinrich Mann, Joseph Roth, Musil or Broch. Contaminating, *the acid and at the same time lucid and clinical look*, can be found in the literatures of the empire's former provinces or in the works of the writers formed in their vicinity (the literary beginnings written in Hungarian of the Romanian author Liviu Rebreanu).

***

Within the history of the narrative Musil's novel irrevocably establishes the formula of the reflexive discourse and decrees the poetics of the *essay-novel*, still fascinated by *totality*, by the creation of a World conceived in all its structures and multitude of components. The "anatomy" and "physiology" of the internal body are privileged: the functions and the implications of the various components. In two of the "sketches" of the posthumous chapters (81 and 82), like a Mephistopheles forced to verify and to sanction, Ulrich directs the secret projects stimulating "the exegeses" of a philosopher, time's "penniless prophet", about the nature of the contemporary universe, about the symptomatic phenomena of History. Musil frequently uses Plato's maieutics; this time, his sister, Agathe, asks the questions on the human categories of time. Ulrich improvises, displaying his skepticism or cynicism, determining the category/concept "about the life-for-and-within-something" (Robert Musil, *Omul fara insusiri*, Bucharest, Univers, 1995), relevant for the time's intellectual bankruptcy. The concept is followed by the reflections of the philosopher Meingast, the suspect prophet admired by Clarisse and Walter, willing and thrilled to listen to himself during a dreadful discourse, "analyzed" by Ulrich with his eternal distrust. The general picture of the elements in the structure of Kakania's ideologies is completed by this provoked "discourse" about academic science, culture, the arts, philosophy etc., like in a panorama of vanities, of the intellectual *kitsch* professed by this philosophing clown: "Because, if you remember what I told you about music, the aesthetic phenomenon does not need any additions besides itself, namely, as a phenomenon it already is that which it can totally be, thus the true realization of the will. (The will does not belong to morality, but rather to aesthetics, it is part of the unjustifiable phenomena). Three conclusions can be drawn from this: the world needs to be justified only as an aesthetic phenomenon; any attempt to establish it morally has failed so far, and we will understand why it had to happen like this. Secondly: our statesmen need, as it was required by Plato's ancient intelligence, to learn music again; and Plato formed his impulses on this matter on the intelligence of the East. Thirdly: only the *systematic exercise of cruelty* remains the means at the disposal of the European peoples brutalized by humanitarianism to regain their powers." (My emphasis added, Musil, 1995).

The posthumous sketches are often more expressive and transparent for understanding the critical and violently polemic perspective on a world ongoing an inescapable decomposition. This is what *The Man without Qualities* examines by choosing a critical spirit that is totally, destructively and irremediably ready for self-destruction, for the projected analysis. Such an "exercise" of using cruelty legislates a mechanism and a dominant feature throughout Musil's book, restating the nature of a society where imposture can attract (Clarisse and Walter are fascinated by the aberrations of Meingast). The writer had been only 23 years old when the idea for the novel had started forming in very vague notes (his "Diary" mentions the year 1903). And on the very day of his death – 15 April 1942 – he was still sketching new chapters, new motifs and metamorphoses of the characters' destiny in the notes (I repeat the word)... *The opening narrative time is also the historic time of the events' development*: the summer of 1913, in the seventh decade of Franz Joseph's reign and thirtieth year of Prussian absolutism (Wilhelm II celebrated thirty years of ruling on Germany's throne). The novel is dedicated not only to Kakania, the Austro-Hungarian Empire, but also to the existence of a history of those nations and mentalities experiencing a relentless process of destruction and disappearance.

The novel's first book, "Part I", opens with a passage on the weather and astronomic forecast for that "fine day in August 1913" (Musil, *The Man without Qualities*, London, Picador, 1997, translated by Sophie Wilkins and Burton Pike; p. 3). However, the *incipit* – not unimportantly for the general tone of the narrator's comments – ratifies only in chapter 5 ("Ulrich") the legitimacy of the "chronicle". The narrator's voice denotes a certain *state of mind*: "*Time was making a fresh start just then* (it does so all the time), and a new time needs a new style" (My emphasis added, Musil, 1997, p. 15). Maybe the phrase used in the French translation – "*temps nouveau*" is more suggestive for the ironic discourse of the narrator, conscious that these "modern times" are actually a sad experience before the ending. Thus, a chronotope is put in, organized between the borders of this empire (K.u.K.) overwhelmed by the heterogeneity of the signs which are part of an extremely complicated mythography: nationalities and the geniuses of football and boxing; inventors and writers; brilliant tenors, science people and imperial councilors, professional officers and nymphomaniacs etc. This is a disoriented and bewildered society, where the lying prophets and the anarchists, the theoreticians of the philosophical and political radicalism, the dubious characters of the salons, the interest for a murderer with evident schizophrenia (Moosbrugger) sharpen the degradation. The *dissertation* tends to take a primary position within the narrative discourse, cultivating the paradoxes and the most unusual diagnostics: "the new spirit" and its phenomenology gradually separate themselves under the sign of irony and banter, of endless trivializing. The sciences and the pseudo-scientists' masquerade; the theory of relativity and the discoveries of Niels Bohr; the materialist philosophy and the innovating spirit in music, psychoanalysis and social psychology all meet in this carnivalesque show of "a new spirit" in a "time of passage" (Ibid., pp. 230, 232). The general concept of knowledge is consequently enforced in the excursus which includes a fusion of elements and references: "Knowledge is a mode of conduct, a passion. At bottom, an impermissible mode of conduct: like dipsomania, sex mania, homicidal mania, the compulsion to know forms its own character that is off-balance. It is simply not so that the researcher pursues the truth; it pursues him. He suffers it. What is true is true, and a fact is real, without concerning itself about him: he's the own who has a passion for it, a dipsomania for the factual, which marks his character, and he doesn't give a damn whether his findings will lead to something human, perfect, or anything at all. Such a man is full of contradictions and misery, and yet he is a monster of energy!" (Ibid., p. 231).

On the backdrop of a discourse in which we find Ulrich's defining elements again, "The Parallel Campaign", with the planned honoring manifestations, associates Clarisse's proposal for a "Nietzsche Year" with the same irony of contrasts and of the all-ruling disorder. Therefore, we are invited to enter the world of this hectic show, interested in a stupid murderer or in the German "mystic" (Hans Sepp); the exacerbated, hysterical nationalism, the "German-Christian" cult and the cult for the blood's purity intensify and outline this fair of all vanities... After all, Musil's universe is expressed, exponentially, in the skeptical, cynical philosophy which is also Ulrich's deeply tolerating philosophy.

The *essayist-narrator* is also a warned *chronicler* and as skeptical as the analyst of the spiritual phenomena; without forgetting to recall Kafka's work, the chronicler selects and inserts into his own work the predicting manifestations: the Balkan war (1913) or, as author of cinematographic diaries, he notes down an airplane's altitude record (we are around the start of World War I), the visit of the French president in Russia or an earthquake in Japan. This is the second part of the novel's Second Book, and the chapter is entitled (according to the meditation on the adventure of the historical events) "Pseudoreality prevails; or, Why don't we make history up as we go along?". The voice of the chronicler is still bantering and disillusioned: "In short, much was happening, there was great excitement everywhere around the turn of 1913-1914" (Ibid., p. 390). And later on: "our history looks rather vague and messy, like a morass only partially made safe for pedestrian traffic, though oddly enough in the end there does seem to be a path across it, that very «path of history» of which nobody knows the starting point." (Ibid., pp. 390-391). A surprising philosophy of history seems to have been inspired by a "revisited" *La scienza nuova* by Vico – a philosophy of history put under the scrutiny of Kant and Hegel and later on, under the scrutiny of the unfriendly contemplation of the History contemporaneous to Musil's hero.

A pastiche created by juxtaposing the chapter titles of the novel's "books" (parts) would be an interesting project given the effects of the layers' succession, of the intrigue's development and of the *narrative climax*. I am most certain that the result would be extremely suggestive for the work's structure and plot. Similar in style to the chapter titles of Grimmelshausen's novel, chapter

86 is entitled: "The industrial potentate and the merger of Soul with Business. Also, All roads to the mind start from the soul, but none lead back again". Although other characters are inserted in the general spectacle of the imperial capital, although the projects for the ceremonies are about to be finished (Diotima, Arnheim, Tuzzi, Stumm von Bordwehr etc.), although famous names are mentioned, from Jesus to Buddha or from Martin Luther to Goethe (the efforts of general Stumm "of ordering the civilians' intellectual world" seemed destined to failure), the events are hastened justifying the skeptical distrust of Ulrich. The *off* voice of the narrator registers: "It was a time when the world was being shaken up in various ways, and those who kept themselves well informed toward the end of the year 1913 lived on the edge of a seething volcano, although the peaceful processes of production everywhere suggested that it could never really erupt again." (Ibid., p. 413).

For the "novelist-researcher", an expert in symptoms and a Cartesian spirit given his definite formation, Ulrich is the interpreter, the *raisonneur* specialist in the social, economic and politic phenomena and processes, appealing to "witnesses" during the trial (the chapter "Speculations on the intellectual bull and bear market") against universal History (this time): "Its really history that has always taken a bearish or a bullish line with all mankind – bearish when it is using trickery or violence, and bullish [...] by trying to have faith in the power of ideas." (Ibid., p. 448). The social organism, the stated relations and the revealing of social and spiritual etiology, the psycho-social pathology and society's rarely exposed movements enter the light of that screen ferociously studied in every detail by Musil's narrator. One of the novel's themes is a demystified world, a world where mankind and its spirituality are aggressed, where the intellect and the good are counterattacked and defeated by the *material* and the *evil* (Ibid., p. 450). "New times", "a new world" and "the new man" (the chapter "The temptation" from the second book) are de-sanctified and stripped phrases, subjected to an unmerciful analysis, accusing the tired expressions – definitely compromised now – on a generous, united mankind, animated by love.

The demonized formulas, unfortunately re-used throughout the 1930s and 1940s, about the race's superiority and Pan-Germanism are the object of bitter reflection. The year 1914 began its tragic career and the narrator's meditation announced the death of millions of people. In a sketch for the chapter "Conversations with Schmeisser", Ulrich determined again, in graver and more skeptic terms, the evolution of the German and exponential groups' public opinion: "Starting with year forty-eight, the year of freedom, and with the founding of the German Empire [...] for the majority of the cultured people politics appeared rather as an atavism than an important problem. Almost nothing could now disclose that behind these external processes which followed their usual development, the spiritual events were already prepared for that loss of form, for that availability to decadence and to the consent to suicide born from the self-disgust, which, all of them, make a state-of-mind vulnerable and probably always form the previous, passive condition of the eras full of great and violent political changes" (Musil, 1995). The commentary, communicated through the chronicler's voice, sets light on the directions of the analysis conducted by Musil and the nature of his "treaty" on the disengagement and fatal disappearance of certain phantoms of History.

***

The correlations – suspected and unfairly accused by Musil – with Hermann Broch's trilogy are more pronounced and at the same time more significant in the representations of Kakania, the empire studied by a "sociologist" doubled by an "anthropologist", opened to the numerous and fertile directions of research. Obviously the "political analyst" cannot be absent, and neither can the "erudite" analyst of the cultural, artistic and, generally speaking, spiritual phenomenon. There are no areas and fields of knowledge left uninvestigated by the novelist converted into a "scientist", a chronicler, a creator of fictional universes, willing to examine or to simply register the symptomatology of an ill organism. Starting with chapter 8 of Part I, Kakania becomes the object of plural research. Councilors, uniforms (a true semiotics of the military uniform can be found in the first book of Broch's trilogy); the "high-ranked civil servants" of the empire (during the "Biedermeier Era"); conventions, masks, double-dealing spirit etc. all unite in the so-called "Patriotic campaign" supported by count Leinsdorf and whose detached and impassible secretary will be Ulrich; *a secretary of the devil*, irrepressibly tempted to interrogate and contemplate (passively) an useless project destined for failure from the very beginning. An empire immobilized by immobility and social conventions; an emperor almost ninety years old who had ruled for seventy - the slogans imagined by his lordship count Leinsdorf inevitably became ridiculous and lacking any finality. The narrator sums up the count's opinions: "In his view, the nations of Europe were helplessly adrift in the whirlwind of materialistic democracy. What hovered before him was an inspiring symbol that would serve both as a warming and as a sign to return to the fold." (Musil, 1997, p. 89).

The spectacle had become, in the eyes of the novelist, a true caricature, not only through the lack of understanding of the ongoing processes (in the absence of any realist perception), but also through the inconsistence of all official measures. The panorama of the puppets, instincts, delusions and illusions is more perceptible through the "center" fixed in Diotima's salons (Ermelinda Tuzzi), with high-ranking officers, bankers (Leon Fischel), prelates, extras for the general plan of the show performed by involuntary actors of a comedy related rather to cheap vaudeville. In the novelist's view, the paradigmatic perspective is able to reveal the deteriorated mechanism of all structures of this empire populated by phantoms of the past. Irony dominates the discourse of the narrator. A chapter from Part I, "Cultural revolution" (in the French translation: "Intellectual revolution"), analyzes phenomena such as the contaminated "fever" of a society assaulted by philosophers of "a new morality" and of "a new humanity" (Ibid., p. 53), deceived by the beginning of a new era ("the magic date of the end of a century and the start of another"), with messages transmitted by disoriented intellectuals unable to adopt a convincing attitude. The narrator tells us that we are in the age ("the magical date") of discoveries; they are called: Nietzsche, Dostoevsky, Van Gogh, other illustrious names, not less disconcerting for various categories of creators in a state of frenzied adventure of knowledge and of staggering potential certainties. Instead of providing potential answers, Kakania lives under the sign of celebrations and self-disillusions before a merciless collapse: "The Planning Committee" for celebrating the seventieth jubilee of the accession of His Majesty Emperor Franz Joseph.

In the country with over-dimensioned bureaucracy, the "empire" of Kafka and his contemporaries, the garrisons and the uniforms, the unbalanced architecture lacking style, the dubious taste for a certain genre of historical novels inspired by very distant times, the nationalities and the pride of some superior officers of not having ever visited a museum or seen a theatre performance represent pages taken from the "file" of numerous repeated anamneses. It is an incredible diagnosis for an organization conceived and interpreted as a form-changing monster. In its grotesque version, Kakania can be "read" thanks to the crude and hyperbolical prose of Jaroslav Hašek; the adventures of Šveik actually recreate the vigorous content of Musil's humor metamorphosed in irony and caustic comments, sharper and more violent than the inquiry that could be found in a treaty documenting an empire's downfall. As I have already stated, the anatomy of this hilarious (but also tragic) organization has the most precise and striking dissection in Kafka's prose, especially in *The Process* and *The Castle*; the adventure of the topographer is the drifting of those intellectuals unkindly observed by Musil. The second book (Part II) distances itself through the comments – apparently it represents the analysis conducted by count Leinsdorf (chapter 107, "Count Leinsdorf achieves an unexpected political success") – dedicated to Kakania's history and evolution: some people's betrayals and advancements; the minorities' status: "In this high circle people were deeply troubled because nothing was happening, troubled by an absence of history, so to speak, and a strong feeling that something must be done at long last" (Ibid., p. 562). The failed and lamentable, barren and dull history of Kakania seems, in the exegesis of the essayist-novelist, a series of deviations from the "normal" events' order: "It was the same as anywhere else in the world, of course, but when God cut off Kakania's credit, He did it in so special a style that whole nations had their eyes opened to the high cost of civilization." (Ibid., p. 576); we gradually witness the diagnosis of a cycle of pathological conditions in a lost and de-sanctified universe. The events succeed one another in an amalgam of truly ubu-esque situations; in Diotima's salons (in the Tuzzi house), the actors obviously do not execute the Rabelaisian performance of the interpreted gargantuan. Count Leinsdorf, general Stumm von Bordwehr, Arnheim (the German industrialist and "philosopher") discuss about the parallel Action and about "The Commission-set-up-for-the-formulation-of-a-special-idea" with a gravity crashed by ridiculousness! I referred to it as such because I took into consideration the proposals of the German and French editions, in order to emphasize the frequency of projects lacking any logic or projects regarding the utopias of an announced finale.

Musil must be read whilst examining the sub-text too; the connotations are multiple and the language is intentionally allusive and ironic, the phrases are multi-semantic and can reveal much more suggestively the nature of this *study of political anatomy and geo-politics*. Kakania of *The Man without Qualities* is a corrupt, paralyzed structure; it is a society in crisis, denounced through the revealing of ridiculousness, of the involuntary farce. The undisclosed interests of some politicians and the illusion – absolutely informed by the events – that the Empire could still play an international role despite the flooding succession of errors depict in Musil's vision an anachronous world, whose outdatedness is revealed in all its compartments. The posthumous chapters, sketches and "studies" (fragments of chapters thus described by the author) enlarge such a perspective - maybe even more violent, more cynical and more aggressive. The state's oversized compartments, the absurd connections and their mechanics *de-composed* by the narrator are amplified in relation to how the trial against the empire develops via the presentation of new witnesses and new facts. Musil's world – the correlations with Kafka's pages are absolutely striking – is "filed" in the same manner as the world of informers: File D – on Diotima; File L – on Leinsdorf.

Musil's spokesperson (accepting of course the narrative convention and the characters' configuration) is, it is well-known, Ulrich. All the characters included in the acting system of the narrative construction exist through the commentary, the "voice" and their deliberate "de-humanization" conducted as in a laboratory research. In general, their destiny follows an identical trajectory. If some deviate from the adopted method, then the characters' biographies reveal features more suggestive for the covered itinerary. The commentator of the French edition published at Seuil, Jean-Pierre Maurel, noted Ulrich's *tragic dominant feature*, the result of his critical intelligence. Undeniably, one can detect the character's tragic substance; actually, it is a matter of *clarity of observation*, its "equal" nature, its inability to choose, to be enthusiastic (a "frozen" character, writes the abovementioned analyst). I feel that Ulrich is destined for an eternal dissatisfaction; a "saved" character, rescued and also accused given his intelligence which is never willing to choose. Despite the data inscribed in this organization (so different from the vast typology of the European literatures of the XX century), there is in Ulrich a pathetic and dramatic living, the effervescence and fervor of a unique love: Agathe, his sister, his greatest love.

From the perspective of other characters (Clarisse and Walter – part of the breed of young, disoriented creators often drawn in the traps of noisy and dubious doctrines), Ulrich is "the man without qualities". Namely, he is the representation of one of the times' symptoms, a *process of inner dissolution*, common to the entire ailing society where the stage is populated by odd figures, repressed instincts, weird and bizarre erotic impulses, a result of unexplainable combinations. For Musil's "studies", the characters are "cases"; this does not mean that they are analyzed or subjected to psychoanalytical investigations; Musil strongly and irrevocably rejects Freud's explanations. On the contrary, the reactions, the states of mind, the choices made by one character or the other are legitimized in a narrated context, in the discourse exposed as if part of a scholarly discussion on issues of general interest: politics, Kakania's situation, social classes, political doctrines. There are bank directors, state secretaries, industrialists, exacerbated nationalist manifestations, anti-Semitism. And above all, there are high-ranking officers, royal councilors, petty philosophers, activists and militants of radical groups, disgraceful impulses revealed and treated with ridicule or all-pervading irony.

Even the mere reading of the chapters' titles strengthens the readers' impression that they are about to witness, like in a vast research rearranged in a narrative structure, the complete study of all the articulations to be found in the mechanism of a society set to discover itself: the monarchy, the imperial bureaucracy, the scholars, the artists, the most humble servants of this community; to sum up, a society placed under the lights of a lucid and rigorous judgment, inoperable with the performed incisions. Exponentially, Ulrich, "the man without qualities", is the author of this *treaty about a drifting system*. Therefore, the character's portrait and substance have a privileged position. Only the perspective is different and the views of certain "actant" players assist the complicated and extremely complex drawing of this example born from the disconcerting diversity of exposed points of view. A mathematician by formation and total devotion, passionate about philosophy, which is however frequently questioned, with reserves and amendments caustically communicated, Ulrich benefits from a true "clinical file": spiritual mobility, plural endowment, "he combines a certain aggressiveness" (Ibid., p. 160); and a bit further on, in chapter 40 "A man with all the qualities, but he is indifferent to them. A prince of intellect is arrested, and the Parallel Campaign gets its Honorary Secretary": a virile, non-sentimental spirit, living an existential double characterized by paradoxical manifestations, often by the antagonism of the opposites, "Ulrich was a man forced somehow to live against himself, though outwardly he appeared to be indulging his inclinations without constraint" (Idem, p. 160). According to Musil's utopia, in a world compared to a *laboratory* (!), Ulrich would have experimented with the idea of man, with solutions for how to become a man "lacking visible directors or theoreticians at the top" (idem), he would have decided, "to become something like *a philosopher king*" (My emphasis added, idem).

Occasionally, the character, having so numerous functions in the narrator's vision, is subjected to an exercise typical of the introspective literature, whereas the speculative and self-referential regime is functional. In such conditions, the questions are extremely insistent, framing in the text the problem of the pale and distanced relations with the world, a world rejected or continuously regarded with suspicion. Because the character receives (sometimes) gargantuan dimensions in the interpretation conferred by the author, then it is natural for the enormousness to generate various portraying signs. For example, Clarisse suggests the proclamation of "an Ulrich Year" (see chapter 82, Part II). According to Arnheim, the German industrialist involved in the fantasist projects of Kakania, Ulrich has "wit", an observation contradicted by other confusing manifestations of the character; Arnheim feels that "it was life that was missing" in Ulrich's face (Ibid., p. 589). Nevertheless, he is unsettled by it: "[...] here was a face almost visibly headed for disaster!" (Ibid., p. 590).

Stretched on dozens of pages, Arnheim's remarks, which are meant to disclose Ulrich's unusual and contradictory personality, create an absolutely original destiny in the XX century literature. As if part of a psychoanalytic exercise, the study transcends it and sets itself in an area where each element constructs through opposition, through the antinomy elements and the usage of the oxymoron. Thus, it acquires the value of a higher creation, lacking any comparison terms. Alien to "the crude acquisitive instinct" and still a realist and lucid spirit, Ulrich is "*a man possessed* who was not interested in possessing anything" (My emphasis added, Ibid., p. 597). Arnheim remembers that Ulrich is not at all a "theorist" but has wit, and "the author" of this detailed examination recognizes his own intellectual and spiritual superiority. A wise, witty (*witzig*) spirit, also having that non-conformism/impertinence (*vorwitzig*) typical of a truly unpredictable personality, and always placed in irreducible antagonisms - this is Ulrich in the eyes of those around Arnheim. The hesitations of the 'analyst' are constantly multiplied and emphasized: "a man entirely given to *theorizing*" (My emphasis added, Ibid., p. 597). It seems that the question is contradicted by the opinions of the same fascinated observer, passionate about this apparently psychoanalytic study. The intuitions are continuously contradicted by a certain un-authenticity of the character, skeptical and always ready to amend the impressions generated by the encounter with him.

In order to discover the "factual" living world, Ulrich is determined to observe not without some *cruelty* (!), with lucidity and realism, with the cruelty of a mathematician (Ibid., p. 645). Furthermore, chapter 116 of the second book contains a fragment suggestive for *the formula of the narrative discourse*: the *essay*, a solution expressive for the incisions in the world experienced by the hero, for *the treaty of anatomy and social anthropology* imagined by the novelist in a work unique for the destiny of the XX century novel; the chapter is entitled "The two Trees of Life and a proposal to establish a General Secretariat for Precision and Soul". Under the sign of the "tree", Ulrich's life (this time, a solution of the self-referentiality) is defined in terms valid for the novel's general structure: "This urge to attack life and master it had always been clearly discernible in him, whether it had manifested itself as a rejection of the existing order or as various forms of striving for a new one, as logical or moral needs or even merely as an urge to keep the body in fighting trim. *And everything that, as time went on, he had called essayism, the sense of the possibility, and imaginative in contrast with pedantic precision*; his suggestions that *history was something one had to invent, that one should live the history of ideas instead of the history of the world*, [...], all these different versions of his thinking, all in their extreme formulations against reality, had just one thing in common: an unmistakable, ruthless passion to influence reality." (My emphasis added, Ibid., p. 646).

The highlighting of *the essayist discourse* is constant in the novel's composition, in the usage of a particular type of narrative voice; the free indirect speech alternates or interferes with the direct, first-person discourse. However, beyond such features of the narration and of the narrator, important is the fact that the novel maintains *the attitude and the regime of ironic discourse*, tempted occasionally by the sub-textual allusive language or by the effect of paradoxes developed by the (now confessed) intelligence and lucidity, by *the cruelty of the analytical look*. The dissection is always present in this manual of anatomy dedicated to the empire, the people and their conditions.

Furthermore, the discourse is seen under its double communicational value: the direct, unambiguous language and the "symbolic" one. Ulrich states the nature of the relations and of the languages: "Now, as he realized that his failure to achieve integration had lately been apparent to him in what he called the strained relationship between *literature* and *reality*, *metaphor* and *truth*, it flashed on Ulrich how much more all this signified than any random insight that turned up in one of those meandering conversations he had recently engaged in with the most inappropriate people. These two basic strategies, the *figurative* and the unequivocal, have been distinguishable ever since the beginnings of humanity." (My emphasis added, ibid., p. 647). The reflection reveals the condition of literature (fictional universe), as well as the condition of logical thinking, of rationalizing (unambiguity) all judgments, all "realities" and processes. Among them, *the alienation phenomenon*, the phenomenon of the human relations' disintegration and de-vitalization is placed on a key position in the meditations of various characters. The confessional acknowledgment of a serious and inevitable solitude changes the readers' optic allowing them to discover in Ulrich a human tortured by anxieties and uncertainty. Thus, it generates the feeling that cynicism, irony, mockery, the taste for paradoxes and for the derisional reliving of meetings with the characters of this play with tragic-comical puppets are all immunization attempts. More exactly, they are self-immunization attempts. "Even though had always assumed that he was only toying with these people [mainly, general Stumm and count Leinsdorf], he suddenly felt quite forlorn among them. He remembered feeling something like it a few weeks or months before, a little puff of Creation's breath asserting itself against the petrified lunar landscape where it had been exhaled; he thought that all the decisive moments of his life had been accompanied by such a sense of wonder and isolation."

(Ibid., p. 650).

As I have already stated, regarding the actantial relation of the characters, Ulrich often associates other data from the pages of his inner biography's massive file; speculative, self-examining, or observed by others and thus adding to the components of this unique portrait in the German literature of the XX century. He is the quintessence of that historic time's World, its vast and heteroclite cosmogony. Walter and Clarisse are two of those characters invited to complete the composition assumed by Musil's "treaty". According to Clarisse, the character's *demonic essence* (in Herman Broch's book, the demonic Bertrand is called "a night demon") is situated close to the other pole – Ulrich's duality being consequently affirmed again: "Do you remember if I've ever told you that you're the Devil? [...] Try to understand, I'm not calling you a poor devil: that's the kind who wants to do evil because he doesn't know any better. You are a great devil: you know what's good and you do the opposite of what you'd like to do! [...] But just because you're a devil you have something of a god inside you, Ulo! A great god. The kind who lies to try to keep from being recognized." (Ibid., p. 717-718). The principle of good and evil, even in Clarisse's paranoid delirium, constitutes a dual, bipolar structure, other than that of a Janus in a world less confused and troubled by the Last Day of Judgment...

The third book of Musil's novel deconstructs in order to increase and to reconstruct on a different scale the symptomatic personality of Ulrich, stirred in analyzing himself or provoking revelations about him. Undoubtedly, Part III, "Into the Millennium (The Criminals)", brings in new aspects and new arguments for a character passionate about the thinking of logicians, and taking Aristotelian logic as a model; by formation, it is a matter of the mathematical logic professed by Ulrich; hence, the nature or resonance of his judgments and paradoxes. Rational criticism does not absolve him of unexpected confessions: the hero admits that "One should love an idea like a woman; be overjoyed to get back to it. And one always has it inside oneself! And always looks for it in everything outside!" (Ibid., p. 977). Oscillating and never embracing a single option, Ulrich swings between facts and ideas, between the "hunger" for bourgeois normality and the abstract game of ideas. The presence of his sister, Agathe, generates a different confessional or auto-analytical niche; actually, the readers' impression is that of a Freudian treatment turned into parody and caricature via numerous self-analytical moments, oversized or willingly complicated through the game of frequently cultivated paradoxes.

***

The third part reveals from the very first chapter ("The forgotten sister") the winding and passionate journey of an incestuous love affair, a devastating love of great epic beauty. In the chapters of this extensive part of *The Man without Qualities* there is a scholarly and delicately filtered erotic tension and an atmosphere of hinted sensuality diffused like in a poem dedicated to the never-fully-discharged love. I believe that Agathe is one of the most accomplished characters – the representation of femininity surrounded by the aura of a unique love, "as a dual aspect of nature" (Ibid., p. 748). The uncontainable attraction, the archetypal nature of this intimacy between two human beings that discover their love are conveyed like in a poem dedicated to the eternal revelation of love. Ulrich's other erotic experiences (Diotima, Bonadea, Clarisse) remain a pale memory in front of this forbidden love; the gradual recognition of the passion, the minute signs, the details, the sensuality of the encounter with Agathe's body, with the perfume of her body create one of the most beautiful stories devoted to a couple, to the androgyny myth, but also to the poem of passionate love lived with supreme intensity. The game of love, the illumination of this state generate "suspensions" via the excursus provoked by Agathe about *the hermaphrodite myth*: Ulrich answers to Agathe's questions by saying that "Nobody knows which of so many halves running around in the world is his missing half." (Ibid., p. 981); in their quest for "oneness", brother and sister experience the excitement and the miraculous mystery of their undeclared love. The shadows and the filtered lights of their intimacy alternate with Ulrich's digressions, – a method of keeping his assumed appeal: "It's not only the myth of the human being divided in two; we could also mention Pygmalion, the Hermaphrodite, or about Isis and Osiris – all different forms of the same theme. It's the ancient longing for a doppelganger of the opposite sex, for a lover who will be the same as yourself and yet someone else, a magical figure that is oneself and yet remains magical [...]." (Ibid., p. 982).

Within the space of German literature, from Goethe to the great writers of the XX century, the fluid of love and the mystics of a fusion through love acquire a supreme vibration in Musil's novel. As in a filter of love, Agathe and Ulrich experience love's desire and ardor, passion and fervor, just like in the great poems of the World. "The dream of being two spirits and one at the same time" is the persistent state of the two, and the novelist registers each movement with sensorial acuity and with undetected care for experiencing the desire, a passionate wakefulness. Chapter 45 of the posthumous registers the climax of sensuality and of the couple's closeness, the discovery of an ardor difficult to suppress. The movement and femininity of the gesture and of the embrace are part of a nuanced and imperceptible passage to the desired "impossible" (Musil, 1993). The memorable page of this erotic experience undoubtedly remains one of the most profound pages in German literature. The interdictions were broken like in a mystical and unique revelation of passion. Obviously, via his character Musil exponentially transcribes a dissertation on love, after the pages where the Eros's exposure transcends the inclination for lucid and cold observation; Chapter 52 (posthumous) gives the occasion for an exposition that maintains the requests and the conditions of an essay on love (Chapter "Conversations about love"). Barely sketched, the chapter seems a scholarly speech given at a conference on love: "Man, or even better said, the speaking animal, is the only one who needs the perpetuation of conversations [...] because his capacity of loving is essentially connected to his capacity of speaking, and in such a mysterious way that it almost reminds us of the ancient whose philosophy believed that God, people and things were born out of the «Logos», which for them meant either the Holy Spirit,

Ration or Speech. Furthermore, neither psychoanalysis nor sociology added anything essential in this regard, although these two of the youngest branches of science challenge Catholicism for interfering with all human domains..." (Ibid.). Such a way of desecrating the experienced moments is related to the work's general vocation and oscillates, often tragically, between gravity, tragic and staging a mechanism characteristic to banter and to the somewhat "frivolous" consideration. However, the game always has a serious element to it. Ulrich's anti-sentimentalism is a mechanism of defense, surveillance and of perceiving the world. The "theoretical" excursus seems contagious; Agathe herself lives the passionate moments observing "the mystical participation" in love (Ibid.). Their love is rendered ambiguous, as part of the same "stage-manager's" method used by the narrator and by Ulrich.

Beyond the gradual evanescence of the senses' intensity, beyond the "dialogue" of the two lovers, brother and sister, "The Siamese twins", the love's ineffability is noted down in "diary" fragments, in which Ulrich clarifies the evolution of their relationship: "Ulrich often thought that what he was experiencing with Agathe was just a reciprocal suggestion and could only be understood as a result of the influence of the thought that an extraordinary destiny had chosen the two of them. This destiny placed them either under the sign of the Siamese twins or under the sign of the Millenary Empire, of the seraphic love or of the myths of the world's «concave» experiences." (Ibid.). The essay-discourse, distinctively reflexive, thus delimiting – given the digressive commentary – the levels of the narrative "body", covers different opinions on love, on its nature, from the ardor and the sensorial outburst to the ineffable erotic game or the ecstatic state generated by love and not by "sentiment" (Ibid.). In an older "study" "sketch" entitled "Hermaphrodite" (chapter 89 of the posthumous), Clarisse makes confessions to the philosopher Meingast, the remarks shifting the discussion to the level of a schizophrenic delirium: "I am not a woman, Meingast! *I am the hermaphrodite!* [...] I will be leaving with you. You will see. I will show it to you on the first night. We will not be a sole being, but you will be two. I can leave myself. You will have two bodies" (Ibid.); the metamorphosis and the deviations are familiar to Musil's essay from the numerous finished chapters or the barely sketched chapters of the posthumous. The oscillations and the alternations of the states of mind, within the extraordinary erotic performance imagined by the narrator, draw a true novel of mystic love incarnated by a supreme vibration of human beings. "Agathe rested on Ulrich's chest, almost loosing her conscience. At that moment she felt hugged by her brother in such a wide, clam and pure embrace like nothing else on earth. Their bodies did not move and had not changed, but were invaded by such a sensual happiness as they had never known. A strange voluptuousness, completely supernatural. There wasn't just a thought anymore and there wasn't imagining anymore! Anywhere they touched each other, on the hips, on the hand or on a lock of hair, they were entering one another." (Ibid.). Ecstatic, the confessed state seems to be the fulfillment of an always-postponed desire; each time, the moments of climax and voluptuousness are followed by a break-up. A necessary break-up, like an interval or a space where – repeated – the states of mind experienced before are elucidated, like in a necessary attempt (cf. Musil, 1993). A mysterious mechanism sublimates the immediate impression, and between the profane and the sacred their love would continue its journey, passionately, discovering an ever more intensified sexuality, with mysterious hours of this scholar song of passion.

The theme, an old theme represented in the works of Greek tragic authors, is reiterated by William Faulkner in *Absalom, Absalom!*, the novel of unique musical structure, where the narrator, Quentin Compson, will record the confessions of the Families from the mythical land of Yoknapatawpha. The script of the second Book of the Kings (chapters 13-14) is recreated on the models acknowledged by the American novelist in other works, starting with his short-stories and continuing with the cycle of the great Families of the South. The narrator and the carriers of confessions in their active memory have the conscience of the tragic destiny, of the *hubris*: "Maybe he knew there was a fate, a doom on him, [...] some things that just have to be whether they are or not, just to balance the books, write *Paid* on the old sheet [...]" (William Faulkner, *Absalom, Absalom!*, Vintage International, 1990; p. 260). Judith Sutpen and Charles Bon, engaged under the impulse of a powerful love, stain with blood the history of this book through the hindering of the incest by Henry Sutpen, Judith's brother, who kills Charles Bon. Because "the stage-manager of this play" – Fate or destiny – decides the tragic development of the events. The demoniac Thomas Sutpen triggers the mechanisms of the tragedy, with numerous references to the characters of the Greek tragic authors. The story of Quentin, who is destined to keep in his memory the events' development, recreates the obsessive images of the people: "[...] he could see it; he might even have been there. Then he thought *No. If I had been there I could not have seen it this plain*" (Faulkner, 1990, p. 155).

Under the sign of recollections and, consequently, under the sign of the *remembering story*, epic histories are transmitted in the novel by Graham Swift *Waterland*: "But *when the world is about to end there'll be no more reality, only stories*. All that will be left to us will be stories. We'll sit down, in our shelter, and tell stories, like poor Sheherazade, hoping it will never..." (My emphasis added, Swift, 1999, p. 298.). The fears and anxieties of the novel's world are metamorphosed in the stories of a teacher in a London college; among them, the tragic story of the Atkinson family: the last offspring of a great family from the water district, Ernest Richard Atkinson, will break the moral law through the incest committed with his own daughter, Helen; a progeny charged by the stigma of the sin is epically relived in this Faulkner-esque work by a British writer devoted to narrative and to History: "The subject is still history" (Ibid., p. 153).

***

The preliminaries of this reading dedicated not only to Robert Musil's novel but also to other narrative creations such as *The Sleepwalkers* - the trilogy by Hermann Broch, the novels by

Kafka, Thomas Mann, Gombrowicz or Günter Grass (the choice can be amended or criticized, as other numerous works could have been called to ratify the alternatives of the novel and, likewise, of the reading) announced the *theoretical* option for the *essay-novel*, for the narrative discourse conquered and always enticed by *reflexivity*. It would however be an error to believe that the author of these comments, a reader of novels not only because they reconfirm and totally certify the supremacy and the condition of being of the narration, confers a privileged position and value to this formula of the novel. In fact, starting with Rabelais's supremely carnivalesque, heteroclite work with variable form, and continuing with *Don Quixote*, with the French novel (Lesage, Diderot), with the great English novelists of the XVIII century (Fielding, Laurence Sterne, Richardson), with Balzac and with the monumental creations (modern given their destinies and themes) of Dickens, Flaubert, Zola, Proust, Joyce, Virginia Woolf, Faulkner, Malcolm Lowry, the Latin-American narrative of great magic realism etc., the novel has continued to be meditation about and history of the human condition, of the destiny of the subjugated and threatened human being. With Franz Kafka, the novel has discovered a different way (that *something else* appreciatively mentioned by Gabriel Garcia Márquez) of looking at the tragic condition of the individual and of humanity.

Therefore, reading Musil and, later, Broch and Günter Grass will take into consideration a certain specificity of the German prose (evidently, other literatures of German expression as well), visibly inclined to reflexivity, to subject the imagined narrative universe to a generalizing examination. Within the same epic space, I also think about Ernst Jünger, in whose work the depth of thought is often expressed via a system of symbols and allegories (*On the Marble Cliffs*, *Heliopolis*, *The Glass Bees* etc.), which he also chooses to use in his diaries. The *essay-novel*, constructed through the full liberation of the thought toward multiple references/digressions and thus accomplished on multiple levels fuelled by the always profoundly-narrative substance, affirms the value of the narrative script and of the epic event assumed via the created fictive universes. Ernst Jünger's *selection* is very resolute: the eulogy of the Bible - a fundamental text and vast epic creation; and *One Thousand and One Arabian Nights* – the Oriental work being an absolute model of human archetypal communication. Since the author of the famous *The Storm of Steel* (one of the most shuddering confessions about World War I) cultivates the thought frequently transposed in metaphor and allegory, the *Logos* presides just like it can be constantly found in *The Man without Qualities*.

The formula of the essay is evident from Musil's first book; a few chapters call out the very solution of the essay: "The first of three attempts to become a great man"; "The second attempt. Notes toward a morality for the man without qualities"; "The most important attempt of all" (I believe that in this context the word's meaning – the Romanian translation is "essay/attempt" – is determined by the specific solutions of the essay as text in which the concentration and selection of some themes, of their circumscription and multitude of connections intended to "place in the abyss" a certain issue, give depth to the genre). Characters and epic situations; events and new strategies in the accumulation of the plot's elements; the organization and continuation of the narrative text's climax, but especially the creation of the ideas' tension demand the essay formula in Musil's prose. The narrator, or the protagonist, grasps moments, debates, dialogues where Plato's maieutics presides over the debates and encourages the discourse typical of the essay. The observation of some characters intentionally caricaturized or set in the light of the unconditional ridicule requests the "improvisation" or, in other words, the essay. In the (sketched) chapter of the posthumous, "Why people are not good, beautiful and truthful, and they only prefer to wish to be like this", the presence of Meingast (the false prophet and the philosopher of deplorable thoughts) and of other characters that illustrate diverse doctrinaire tendencies triggers the taste for essayistic dissertation on the life "for-and-in-something" (Musil, 1993); other times, suggesting diagnoses for the foggy movements of the times' ideas. Furthermore, the discourse continues to ridicule and to disassemble some philosophical aberrations (Meingast) and it becomes, obviously, an essay fragment;

the same Meingast conveys his ideas about a society with "a new order", about the fall and collapse of the bourgeois civilization, about "a new structure", "a new force concentration", situated in the proximity of a Nazi philosophy (Schmeisser): "The pseudo-heroic individualism and liberalism have gone bankrupt..." (Ibid.).

An interesting fact is that the vocabulary is taken from the linguistic national-socialist arsenal and the props are not foreign to the fascist doctrines examined here with lucidity and extraordinary intuition by this great novelist. Hence, the role given to certain representations significant for a sick world, invaded by an incurable pathology, also endemic given its nature. The pages devoted to a visit to a mental institution are memorable; the guide is General Stumm von Bordwehr. Actually, it is a first encounter with the Inferno, an inferno which predicts the deplorable ending of a suffering humanity. Some of the most surprising reasons are associated and placed in paradoxical, absurd relations in the anti-chamber of dementia: politics, the monarch, the empire, whereas the spectators are General Stumm, Ulrich, the doctor and Clarisse, she herself, as I have already mentioned, an absolutely obvious clinical case: "In this new ward a series of horrible apparitions crouched and sat in their beds, everything about their bodies crooked, unclean, twisted, or paralyzed. Decayed teeth. Waggling heads. Head too big, too small, totally misshapen. Slack, dropping jaws from which saliva was dribbling, or brutish grinding motions of the mouth, without food or words. Yard-wide leaden barriers seemed to lie between these souls and the world, [...]. Such wards for severe mental deficiency are among the most horrifying sights to be found in the hideousness of a mental institution, [...]." (Musil, 1999, p. 1096). Instead of the general, Dr. Friedenthal accompanies Clarisse to the darkness of this inferno painted in the expressionists' hard lines and strong touches. The sight of the idiots, their world that attracts Clarisse, triggers the narrator's comment which hints to the most unexpected sub-textual suggestions: "Hell is not interesting, it is terrifying. If it has not been humanized – as by Dante, who populated it with writers and other prominent figures, thereby distracting attention from the technicalities of punishment – but an attempt has been made to represent it in some original fashion, even the most fertile minds never get beyond childish tortures and unimaginative distortions of physical realities." (Ibid., p. 1070).

The obsession of such scenes worthy of the frightening visions of Hieronymus Bosch or Bruegel returns constantly in the works written during this German or Austrian "age", an age of premonitions or of intuitions situated beyond the strictly lucid or "scientific" analysis of the events. In the trilogy by Hermann Broch (in its first part), the imminent death of "mister" v. Pasenow, assisted by a neurologist and watched – without too much excitement – by Joachim, is an extraordinary exercise of analyzing the demented senility as never before encountered in the XX century literature.

***

The Man without Qualities confirms, in its vast proportions, the project designed by Musil; beyond his intentions and beyond the unfinished pages (they nevertheless give a suggestive representation of the incomplete structures), Musil's novel reaches one of the conditions of the last century's narrative: *the totality, the World as totality*, seen in all its manifestations and functional structures, like in a study in which the research instruments come from a multidisciplinary examination: anthropology and sociology, psychology and political science, ideology, doctrinarian directions and a philosophy of history – all of which are conjugated in multiple relations; the other components of this totalizing structure are not missing either: culture and the arts, inter-human relations, their deterioration etc. To sum up, an all-inclusive vision presides over Musil's writing, and the *essay-novel* justifies the mobility, the reflexivity and the meditation's whimsical itineraries. Among others, this is one of the explanations provided for the writer's obvious preference for the effect of digressions, commentaries and diagnoses pictured from the perspective of an involved but still detached observer: Ulrich – an ironic observer, not condescending at all, pleading for the revealing of the studied phenomena and their inclusion into the ironic, acid or caustic discourse, sometimes tempted to appeal to the absurd through ridicule and its mechanics. The narrator calls such *anamnesis exercises* and – later – *diagnosis exercises* "Speculations on the intellectual bull and bear market" (the title of chapter 91 of the second part of the second book); in the previous chapter, the comments deal with "dethroning of the ideocracy" and with devaluing the spirit's territories. The provocative and constantly inciting dialogue with Arnheim directs the discussion towards literature and, in general, towards the creator's status: Trying to animate the discussion and to steer it on to a less conformist course, Ulrich raises the question: "It boils down to the naïve question Why do professional storytellers write? *They write about something that never happened as if it had actually happened, obviously*" (My emphasis added, ibid., p. 453). Dissimulating and playing his part till the end, Ulrich ridicules the soirée discussions (Arnheim, Tuzzi), accepting that "much as it troubles" him, he was never tempted to write; the alleged aesthetics was common in those times and it was rather likely to trivia-lize the assertions. And nevertheless, the creator comes out like a "thief" of happiness through the created imaginary. The game interpreted by Ulrich goes on in the chapter "The great man of letters: rear view"; the theorizing excursus continues with reflections on "the great man of letters", the publisher, and literary criticism: "His publisher stops saying that a businessman who goes into publishing is a sort of tragic idealist, because he could do so much better for himself by dealing in textiles or unspoiled paper. The critics discover him as a worthy subject for their labors, because the critics are often not really bad people at heart but former poets who, because times are bad, have to pin their hearts to something that will inspire them to speak out; [...]." (Ibid., p. 468). From Ulrich's point of view, neither "the front view" (the following chapter) changes the adopted perspective: all the components – I already noted it – of society are affected by the corrosive, unforgiving, demystifying action of the narrator tortured by the sight of a World in straight downfall!

In the end, the impression is that the writer invents a learned, perfectly informed and reasoned "physiology" of the creator - "the great man of letters"; as the narrator notes with sad irony, he "has his place in the days of great political campaigns and great department stores" (Ibid., p. 466), continuing to obliterate the portrait, connected to that of Thomas Mann in *Death in Venice*: Gustav (von) Aschenbach in full crisis, discovering his false image as a "Great writer" publicized by his contemporaries. Musil proceeds similarly by demolishing the myth of the writer "acknowledged" by textbooks and critics, who are themselves contaminated by the same infection of the time and of its pillars: the wars and "the department stores". The author of *The Man without Qualities* rediscovers the taste for caricature from Grimmelshausen's picaresque work or does not forget that Thomas Mann observes the behavior and the states of mind of a creator such as Goethe in *Lotte in Weinmar*, without the unforgiving accents of Musil's work. How vast and diverse are the comments of the participants to these prolonged Platonian colloquies on the condition of arts and of the artist in an agitated contemporary society, traumatized by many phenomena widely aggravating for the individuals. The cinematograph at his beginnings; the imagination of the creators and the influence... of the great companies (A.E.G., Deutsche Farbenwerke (Arnheim warns that there will emerge an art of the great companies); thus, the great electrical corporations and the industry of colorants are observed by an industrialist (probably as skeptical as his interlocutor, Ulrich); they devalue art and turn it into a "consumer's" product – as we call it today –, anticipated by Musil as symptom of the degradation of all society's constituents, and not only of Kakania's constituents.

***

The said monologue, presented in a rhetoric typical of the exposition of certain motivations, or meant to respond – indirectly – to some affirmations, is conjugated in the narrative discourse with the essay and, through its solutions, with digressions; they broaden themselves, I suppose, through associations of ideas and references set in motion by the characteristic props of examples, phenomena or causes, *a branched development of digressions*. Their frequency and technique are extraordinary in Musil's novel; as I have stressed it before, there are no structural fields or phenomena that are left outside the ideas' active zones, full of emergency: religion, philosophy, politics, morality, "bourgeois culture", the manifestations of Catholicism, the effects of the baroque, the illicit fortunes or fortunes made thanks to suspicious successional documents etc. Irony is sovereign in the always transformed "views", brought to the eyes of the actants and of the reader. However, the irony of the book's hero is not a mere derision; the treatment is far more ruthless and it registers the diagram of an irreversible and definite process of *dissolution* and of inexorable dissipation of the moral values. The formula is less characteristic in chapter 48 ("The three causes of Arnheim's fame and the Mystery of the Whole"), where the portrait of this industrialist-philosopher, 'Vatican-like representative' of the great industrialists, is made up of numerous and infinite references to all sorts of different fields ("[...] one need only imagine the effect of Maeterlinckian or Bergsonian philosophy applied to questions about the price of coal or to cartel politics, [...]." (Ibid., p. 206). Naturally, the narrator surveys not only through his comments but, implicitly, suggests a *parody game* and an unseriousness aimed at dethroning such often-redundant assertions, verging on ridicule. We could 'cut out' several essays as autonomous structures about "a two-headed god or the devil's cloven hoof" (Ibid., p. 307), embarking on lengthy comments (Ulrich) on the evil's myths, on modern psychology; individualism and collectivism, pacifism, nationalism etc. A chapter from Part I is designed as an essay on Evil and chapter 83 ("Pseudoreality prevails; or, Why don't we make history up as we go along?") is focused, essayistically, on the World as a discourse about the world, as it could be entitled. In this case, the composition is obviously essayistic, casual through digressions ("digression one", "digression two", "digression three"), according to rhetoric standards tempted to discuss the great problems of the World.

The insertion of the most symptomatic manifestations of society in such an epic construction realizes *a true phenomenology of the social and of the spirit*, of the sciences and of philosophy, radically amended, although elements of psychoanalysis are to be found in the study of behaviors subjected to an intense exploiting examination. Not less significant are the meditations about the alienated human being and about the "sane" one (?), about religion - Ulrich's ideas having been inspired by the most surprising doctrinaire directions. A skeptic and displaying non-conformism with some ostentation, Ulrich proclaims his own convictions: "I don't believe that God has been here yet, but that He is still to come. But only if we pave the way for Him more than we have so far!" (Ibid., p. 1109); as regards morality, Ulrich disputes that it "arises through force and violence! A group of people that has seized power simply imposes on the rest those rules and principles that will secure their power." (Ibid., p. 1112). As it can be noticed, the sources are no stranger to Marxism, and sometimes to the most contradictory and even peripheral directions. The taste for the often ostentatious stating of paradoxes is cultivated and surveyed; it depends of course on the interlocutors as well, and on the motivations of some demonstrations framed as such: the alienated and the sane; the Marxist theses, presented in totally original and caricaturing interpretations; the ambiguous nature of the individual; the genius and the imbecility of men; the *paradox* dominates and Ulrich cultivates it not without delight or humor: "The men of genius race or the geniuses don't even have to be geniuses actually. He, the so admired genius, is born only at the Vanity Stock Market; in his brilliance the mirrors of the surrounding stupidity find their brilliance; he is always connected to something that gives him prestige, as well as money and honors; and no matter how big his merit is, in reality, his phenomenon is just a stuffed geniality... (Musil, 1993). It needs to be said that Agathe's presence stimulates such reflexive demonstrations, typical of Musil's spirit, assumed through his main character and reaching the witticism on "the leading spirits" chosen from among Plato's disciples, in a succession that could have become fatal... ("God took action with all precaution when He ordered an elephant to give birth only to an elephant and a cat only to a cat; however a philosopher gives birth to a parrot and a counter-philosopher!", ibid.).

The played game of the essay and digression continues, and it even widens from one "book" to the other, like in the case of the beliefs conferred to the "genius". The posthumous Chapter 49 is entitled, as a continuation of the amusing consideration from the previous chapter, "General von Stumm on geniality"; he pushes the rigid vision on the genius towards the enormous; by condemning the "chaos created by the existence of so many geniuses among civilians" (Ibid.), the general registers – without any complexes – the explanations given by psychoanalysis and the theory of relativity. By stimulating him in the asserted absurdities, Ulrich summons examples (obviously foreign to the general) of great creators, continuing with an impressive demonstration of an authentic scientist, disappointed and skeptical; an untreatable skeptic in the end. Sophocles, Mozart, Bach, Goethe, Einstein give testimony in a discussion constructed according to the rules of maieutics, slightly parodied nevertheless, but with accents of serious meditation. Ulrich's answers are controlled not only by logic, but also by the pathetic features of the examples' eloquence: "«One hears the first notes from Bach or Mozart; one reads the first page from Goethe or Corneille and one knows that he reached geniality!»" (Ibid.). I have said that Ulrich's discourse is controlled and surveyed by logic, a study object for the character who also studied the fields of science (the biography of Robert Musil registers the same plural formation). The reflections follow the way the interlocutor formulates vague objections or asks questions. The logician however, not forgetting that he is also a *story-teller* (he tells Agathe about his discussion with general Stumm about the genius), places the explanation in a suggestive generalizing representation: "Sure, a genius has to be *significant* at the same time; because a genius is that superior and full of *significance* reality materialized in certain exceptional circumstances; however, *significant* and important does not only apply to what is rare, but to the universal as well. [...] Because terms like *significance* and *significant* already have, just like all the widely used terms, more meanings" (My emphasis added, ibid.). The discourse thus becomes an exposition on *thought* and *knowledge*, drawing the attention on the representations' nature. In similar fragments from the posthumous, the construction is typical of a thinker who forgets repeatedly to use irony! "Files", "studies" and "sketches" are the names of the posthumous chapters. Nevertheless, the irony or the ironic sentence return in the various dialogues (Stumm - Ulrich), for the delight of a provocative and derisive Ulrich: "The spirit doesn't suit but very limitedly those who govern and rule" (Ibid.).

Absolutely Rabelaisian, chapter 82 ("From a sketch", entitled "Schmeisser and Meingast") disserts, often aberrantly and chaotically, invoking Nietzsche, Goethe, Plato, Lessing, Voltaire, Marx, Napoleon etc., about the future world, about the "mythical times" or about the creative power of mankind (Ibid.).

Thus, the essay is established as dominant style, "managing" the reflexive itineraries of the narrator-Ulrich, "distributing" and throwing the traps for the representation of Kakania to become all-encompassing according to the mentioned novel's model, globalizing in its significant structures. Under the sign of inter-textuality and of multiple interferences of paradigmatic layers, under the sign of confluences and the interaction of the novel's depth levels, *The Man without Qualities* builds up the times' environments with their disillusions, failures or brilliances etc. Without forgetting that starting with the end of the XIX century and until the 1920s and 1930s Vienna became a spiritual centre, totally dominant in literature, music or painting. Obviously, the values are not necessarily those ratified by the authorities of the empire crushed under the burden of bad taste (the architecture for example) in various creative branches (the dilettantism). However, the excursus throughout art history is suggestive: Bach, Wagner, Goethe, Hein, Lev Tolstoy, Stefan George, Fichte, Nietzsche, Grillparzer etc., and the description of the "modern times" needs to be remembered: "The general tendency among the avant-garde in those days was in favor of taking action; people who lived by their brains felt it incumbent upon themselves to take over the leadership from those who lived for their bellies. There was also something known as Expressionism. Nobody could say just what it was, but the word suggests some kind of squeezing-out; constructive visions, perhaps, but inasmuch as the contrast with traditional art revealed them as being destructive, too [...]" (Musil, 1999, p. 493). And here, the subjacent comment nuances and delimits itself from apparent eulogies or from comments borrowed in a simulated way, whereas in numerous other situations the hero unties the troubled environment of Kakania to reach the absurd and the mocking exposure of some aberrant assertions (Hans Sepp and the confusions professed as some revolutionary doctrines, confusions of a right-wing Pan-Germanism and radicalism).

The incursions in the most diverse ages and epochs suit the intellectual mobility of the narrator and the created atmosphere because, it needs to be emphasized, there is in Robert Musil's work an *atmosphere created through the effect of... the ideas and through the suppleness of their approach*. Ulrich and Agathe think of Stendhal and Dostoevsky; of Nietzsche and the inner freedom; of Novalis or Maeterlinck, Kant, Wieland. They are part of this panoptic miraculously created by the narrator, of a game of the ideas, of the never-condescending limitations (see general Stumm interpreting Nietzsche!...).

***

In search for a novel formula related, essentially, to the tradition of the German prose and to the severe and non-conformist tradition of the Reform, Musil advances, indirectly of course, his conception about the novel. The meta-textual elements can be illuminated although the tendency for bantering, for adopting the solution of the ambiguity game is always present. The sub-mediocre novel (Rachel, Diotima's servant, was fulfilling her education using the novels abandoned by her mistress) is read with delight (see Part I, Chapter 41 - "Rachel and Diotima") and the narrator deconstructs the time's models not without sarcasm. Arnheim's discourse in front of a conquered and fascinated Diotima is retained with evident ironic accents because the majority of the assertions relate to common places known at the time (Part

I, Chapter 49 – "Antagonism sprouts between the old and the new diplomacy"). Chapter 62 of the novel's second part, "The earth too, but especially Ulrich, pays homage to the utopia of essayism", registers in a few pages the nature of the character and the practically miraculous attraction for the *essay*: "There was something in Ulrich's nature", notes the narrator in indirect speech, "that in a haphazard, paralyzing, disarming way resisted all logical systematizing, the single-minded will, the specifically directed drives of ambition; it was also connected with his chosen term, "essayism", even though it contained the very elements he had gradually and with unconscious care eliminated from that concept" (Ibid., p. 273). And after a few other considerations, Ulrich mentions the essentials for the evil's nature and essence: "[...] an essay is rather the unique and unalterable form assumed by a man's inner life in a decisive thought" (Idem). Therefore, the *literary model* of the essay professed in the narrative discourse of Musil's work is not excluded nor eluded; and simultaneously, the novelist allows himself to include reflections on the novel's condition in a chapter important for the mechanism of the self-referentiality in which the work's hero is involved. In the chapter "Going home" (Part II), the soliloquy records Ulrich's thoughts, embracing several judgments on the narrative's condition and especially on that of the *novel*: "And in one of those apparently random and abstract thoughts that so often assumed importance in his life, it struck him that *when one is overburdened and dreams of simplifying one's life, the basic law of this life, the law one longs for, is nothing other than that of narrative order* [...]" (My emphasis added, ibid., p. 708). Ulrich notices that the time's movement, the duration and miracle of temporal development within the novel, "stringing all that has occurred in space and time on a single thread" according to the laws of epic account - "that celebrated «thread of the story», which is, it seems, the thread of life itself" - are privileges of the novel because the invented worlds, the fictive worlds invite one to recreate them, the men themselves being "story-tellers" (Ibid., p. 709).

The more or less "serious" approach to literature's forms and their continuous relation with the condition of an agitated and uncertain self within one's intimate reality, are not isolated in *The Man without Qualities*, but the secret of Musil's creation is not apparent from such reflections; it reveals itself gradually and obstinately to the reader willing to return over the pages of this book, a grave and threatening book given its warnings. As I have said it before, Musil's work springs from the German philosophic thinking, from its tension, but also from the revolted and austere spirit of Martin Luther or from the skeptical thinking of Georg Christoph Lichtenberg. The lucidity and depth of the ideas are inspired by this territory of the Idea. "There where the eye unclearly sees", notes Lichtenberg, "begins the realm of death; where there is no clear imagine, there is no representation". This is one of the defining motifs of this creation (Georg Christoph Lichtenberg, *Aforisme*, Bucharest, Univers, 1970).

The experiences of lucidity. The experiences of drama

"What would have been the use of such a thing?! the poet is powerless,
he does not have the power to mend any evil; he is listened to only
when he praises the world, not when he depicts it as it is.
Only lying brings glory, not knowledge!"

"[...] they had erased almost everything which was anyway part of them,
stripping themselves with real pleasure and keeping only their blind pride
in a crepuscular greed, in a crepuscule full of greed"

(Hermann Broch, *Moartea lui Virgiliu*, Editura Paralela 45, 2003)

It seems that the friendship between Elias Canetti and Hermann Broch was far stronger and more generous as regards their discussions on creation and on the writer's condition. It explains the numerous notes to be found in Canetti's memoirs volumes, notes filled with opinions extremely significant for the diagram of the time's ideas and for the options of the two novelists. In *The Play of the Eyes* (Bucharest, Dacia, 1989), the dialogue is substantial concerning a potential poetics, and especially a poetics of the novel; its forms are analyzed from the perspective of the imperatives of the historic and aesthetic time.

Elias Canetti considered the trilogy by Hermann Broch, *The Sleepwalkers*, "*an atmosphere work*". It is a totally accurate remark given the evolution of the characters and the increasingly dramatic tension of the events. Assuming the information given by the memoirist, it is interesting to note that Broch was an admirer of Freud, fascinated, just like a disciple, by the conception and terminology of psychoanalysis; Canetti tells us that the writer was "fascinated by Freud, in a religious way I might say [...], he was imbued by Freud like by a mystic teaching" (Canetti, 1989), placing the scholar in the same family with Kant, Spinoza or, supreme appreciation, with Plato! With regard to the forms of the modern novel, contemporary to the writer, the memoirist reassures us that Broch was aware of the fact that in Joyce's time the nature of the genre was being transformed radically (a *different* novel!), imagining new destinies and gaining *a new narrative substance* (cf. Canetti, 1989).

Having a biography somewhat similar to that of Musil, the author of *The Sleepwalkers* belongs, as Milan Kundera highly suggestively asserts, to a time dominated by "monsters" generated by an agitated History ready to explode. Kundera believes that the "inner monsters" were the privilege of writers such as Proust or Joyce; that was the time of a generation that went through harsh and tragic experiences: "It is less in his philosophy of history than in this new way of seeing the man (seeing him under the celestial arch of the ages), that Broch in *The Sleepwalkers* prefigures, I think, the future possibilities of the novel." (Kundera, 2000, p. 55). In the third part of the abovementioned volume of essays, Kundera, author of *Immortality* among other admirable books, dedicates to Hermann Broch a consistent chapter – "Notes inspired by «*The Sleepwalkers*»". The Czech writer will extrapolate the Broch phenomenon via wider considerations on the nature of contemporary narrative poetics, a territory conclusively enriched by novelists like Musil and Broch. Remembering to emphasize, and thus detaching himself from the theoreticians of literary sociology, that the novel – given its aesthetic status – remains an explorer of life, rejecting the forms' "specialization" according to the model advanced by sciences and by other fields of knowledge, the author of *The Art of the Novel* invokes Broch's model: "In the age of the excessive division of labor, of runaway, the novel is one of the last outposts where man can still maintain connections with life in its entirety." (Ibid., p. 67).

One cannot contest Kundera's choice when he declares the absolute supremacy of Kafka's work in that *something else*, as exploring universe, as dismemberment of all sick joints of the World, deconstructing and illuminating in the name of a *view* burnt by the desire to discover those areas of the conscience and of the inner time, of the hidden freedom of humanity that had remained forbidden until then. Historically speaking, Kafka's merit exceeds the authority of that period of psychologism in narrative; in essence, there were not that many works in the inter-war literature that re-discovered the dramatic quality of existence, the events with serious consequences for the World's ontology. A different way of investigating and of knowing will be discovered by the Europeans through the works of William Faulkner, Ernest Hemingway, Gertrude Stein, John Steinbeck, John Dos Passos, Erskine Caldwell. When in 1946 Maurice-Edgard Coindreau publishes a panorama of the American prose, *Aperçus de la literature américaine* (Gallimard), The French critics and readers knew too little about this literature of mythical universes, of a great clash between passions and consciences. A literature of harsh conflicts and truly magical territories forces itself, re-positioning the performance of fictional universe. Something similar had happened in the XIX century when the works of Gogol and Tolstoy, Turgenev and Chekhov, Goncearov and above all Dostoevsky had started to be acknowledged. Finally, the literary cosmos experiences after the Second World War the revelation of the Latin-American prose, received in all its great diversity: Jorge Luis Borges, Bioy Casares, Gabriel Garcia Marquez, Llosa, Cortazar, Pablo Neruda, Alejo Carpentier, Roa Bastos etc.

The reference moment of greatest resonance remains thus, Franz Kafka; I believe that in *The Castle* are concentrated the most dramatic and tragic existential themes regarding the altered and devalued destiny of the individual, stripped of all conventions and illusions of an Utopia definitely compromised now.

Given the way Musil, Broch or Witold Gombrowicz (in a direction initiated astonishingly) seem to follow the perceptible signs of Kafka's message, I will define – as I have already tried in the case of Robert Musil – the characteristics of the vision and of the narrative discourse as: *reflexivity*. Each novelist who was part of the family of writers attracted by the idea and by the meditation projected on events and destinies has the very confident and undeniable conscience of the creation able to communicate according to a specific language, without equivalents in other fields of knowledge: "The novelist", writes Kundera in the poetics/the poetic art dedicated to the genre, "is neither historian nor prophet: he is an explorer of existence" (Ibid., p. 44). The *leitmotif* of these writers originating in a space historically and geographically circumcised to the days of the inexorable crepuscule of the Empires is the *disintegration*, the *decomposition* and, finally, the *disappearance*. It is the end of an era, forecasting dark clouds and serious quakes. Hermann Broch embraces *an age of the individuals, a tragic hour of the disintegration of values* (cf. Kundera, 2000). Common themes and motifs inscribed in this space-time also determine a common type of fictionalization of the World: *the essay*.

The formula *reflexive-novel* (*essay-novel*) rejects the monotony or the monotoned discourse; the reality is that the novel's forms astonish through the unusual solutions, infiltrated in the narrative discourse: the digression, the analytic space, the *setting into abyss*, the focus and the self-referentiality, the *song*, the game of the modalities' alternation, the *play of figures and masks*, the pseudo-biographies and the incision in one of the characters' existential dominant features, the anamorphous (numerous and brilliant given their effect). Here is a group of elements conjugated and orchestrated in what I could call the novels' often musical composition. Kundera seems not to overrate the forms of this polymorph novel, protean by transcending certain acknowledged limits: he names the novel alternative "gnosiological" and/or "polyhistorical", without forgetting to mention that these terms were actually first designated by the author of *The Sleepwalkers*!

We realize how resistant and open such novel alternatives are by examining the experience of several post-war German writers. The post-war prose (following the defeat of the Third Reich) remains faithful to the experiences of such novelists as Musil and Broch; it takes over the taste for digressive comments, for irony and parody, for the reflection typical of the narrator and of his voices. Moreover, several elements of visualization and of staging the grotesque, the tragic and the tragic-comic; the reaffirmation of a world undergoing a process of degradation but also of illumination of consciences are to be found in Günter Grass or Heinrich Böll (*The Clown*, *House without Guardians*, *The Lost Honor of Katharina Blum* and his short-stories). It is an enlightening fact that generally the majority of the writers united in "Group 47" follows the same narrative directions. Very suggestive are also the dramatic works of Friedrich Dürrenmatt or Max Frisch, both coming from the Swiss space.

There is nothing unusual in the evolution of Musil's and Broch's novels when we relate them to their model – Kafka, and subsequently, to the other admired writers: first and foremost, Joyce, and as regards Hermann Broch, the name of André Gide also needs to be added.

The reader will notice that I included in this analysis works of German expression beyond the geo-political borders valid at the beginning of the XX century or today; it does not however mean that the Austrian literature (during the Empire) had not produced unique characteristics. They can be distinguished thematically and within the genre of discursive methods, and I will leave it to that. Nevertheless, it is a matter of thematic dominant features and of a located problematic, not taking into account the borders of the evolution (historically speaking) of the literature written in German. Returning to the environment typical of Vienna, significant are the judicious observations of the German literary historian, Fritz Martini, which I have already referred to in my comments devoted to Robert Musil. The former student of Julius Petersen (the famous Berliner professor, author of the paper "*Die Wissenschaft von der Dichtung. System und Methodenlehre der Literaturwissenschaft*") significantly examines the frequency of certain motifs found in the works of the aforesaid writers, and he associates them with the very diverse creation of Hugo von Hofmannsthal. The play-writer ("he transliterated the tragedies of Sophocles in the area of the *obsessive demonic*"; my emphasis added, Martini, 1972) and the novelist, too observe and interrogate a drifting system and a drifting world, the twilight of a world and of a culture. Traumatized, but keeping their balance and their sight clear, the epoch's writers are the prophetic voices of a world which continues to proclaim serious endeavors, the writers being followed by the authentic literary consciences of the end of the XX century and the beginning of the XXI century.

Indeed, Musil's great themes are paramount in Broch's trilogy: the spiritual crisis, the intellectuality and its reaction to the foretelling signs of this Spengler-like twilight of the Kakania Empire, as well as the severity and depth of the sight of the analyst-novelist, an interpreter of society – a society humanized not through the characters' structure and reactions, but through the message transmitted by the novelist not indifferent to the future of the World. For R.-M. Albérès, Broch's novel is a true examination of the "infra-human comedy" surveyed by the analyst-novelist, condemned to reveal the vices of a seriously ill society or, to be more precise, of a society meant to disappear. The literary historian asserts that Broch's world is unable to wake up from what I would call a pre-comatose state, which could be lasting... (cf. R.-M. Albérès, 1969, pp. 206-207).

***

The Sleepwalkers, "the trilogy novel", dates from 1931-32 and it is made up of "The Romantic" ("*Pasenow oder die Romantik (1888)*"); "The Anarchist" ("*Esch oder die Anarchie (1903)*"); "The Realist" ("*Huguenau oder die Sachlichkeit (1918)*") - three titles for the three parts, familiar expressions for the readers of XVIII century novels. I have referred to Broch's great passion for James Joyce; even when he wrote *The Sleepwalkers*, Broch devoted himself to several conferences about the author of *Ulysses* and in 1936 he wrote the essay "James Joyce and actuality". It is also true that *Ulysses* (published in 1922) enjoyed, ten years after the first violent reactions against the book, a relatively more favorable status; however, this does not mean that it compelled final recognition in the literary world of writers and critics. As regards the readers, *Ulysses* was still a novel without significant echoes. In 1929, at the initiative of Adrienne Monnier, "a «Ulysses» lunch" was organized close to Versailles, thus marking the publishing of the French edition, as well as the value of Joyce's masterpiece, acknowledged in the French intellectual environment. There were present, among others: Eduard Dujardin, Paul Valéry, Phillippe Soupault, Jules Romains, Sylvia Beach and Samuel Beckett! (cf. James Joyce, *Corespondența*, Bucharest, Univers, 1983).

Joyce's correspondence, which I already made reference to, captures one of the most evocative confessions for understanding his great work; it relates to the intention of the novelist and to the perfectly legitimized structure of *Ulysses*. Before quoting from one of his letters of 1920, I will point out that Broch's affinities, confessed in the essays and his discussions with friends, are understandable given the genre of his narrative project and general vision. Here is Joyce's epistolary fragment: "I've been working on this book for the past seven years – damn it! It is also some sort of encyclopedia. My intention is to set the myth *sub specie temporis nostri*. Each adventure (namely, each hour, each organ, each art being interconnected, interrelated within the structural system of the whole) has not only to determine but also to create its own technique. Each adventure is, to put it like this, a person, although it is made up of several persons, just like D'Acquino talks about the celestial armies." (Joyce, 1983)

Because I address the issues of the essay-novel and of the free discourse, open to digressions and comments, I believe that it is not meaningless to inform the readers about the echoes of Joyce's works in the Romanian critique and prose. The history of the Romanian novel preserves (see G. Călinescu, *Istoria literaturii române de la origini până în prezent*, Bucharest, Minerva, 1982) the experience of Ion Biberi and his novel *Proces* ("Process", 1935), but the echoes of Joyce are also present in the literary critique with numerous comparative references. The role of Mihail Sebastian has to be mentioned, author of an article about James Joyce, published in the magazine "*Cuvantul*" in 1929, seven years after the publishing of *Ulysses* which raised such agitated reactions. The Romanian novelist detects the radical transformations professed in the novel; the absence of the anecdotic ("[...] however, Joyce's writing distances itself with precision from everything known to us"); it is a profoundly original work as regards its structure and "material". And here is another extremely important observation concerning the correspondences and interferences following the publishing of Joyce's book: "The process of writing identifies itself with the process of thinking", notes Sebastian admiringly, just like Hermann Broch will later on (see Mihail Sebastian, *Eseuri. Cronici. Memorial*, Bucharest, Minerva, 1972).

If for Joyce the work of Ibsen is object of enthusiast comments (his first essay analyzes the drama *The Master Builder*) and if the character exists as structural reference for the general construction of the epic work, *Ulysses* offers Broch a model with an exemplary function. Thus, springs the relation, decreed in the three parts of *The Sleepwalkers*, between the three characters and the dates marked in the German titles: 1888 and the role of Pasenow; 1903 and the projection of the character Esch coming from the shadow of Luther; and the year 1908 associated to Huguenau. T. S. Eliot (cf. Jean Paris, *Joyce par lui-même*, Éditions du Seuil, 1957) drew attention on Joyce's intention (a "demiurgic" intention) of entering the universe of his characters to give a universal meaning to their relations and evolution, like in a *Divine Comedy* shaken by the manifestations of the tragic. It almost feels like we are listening to the voices of the Third Canto of the *Inferno* talking about "the wicked seed of Adam" and how "Charon, demonic spirit, with his eyes / of burning coal, collects them with a sign" (Dante Alighieri, *The Divine Comedy*, Anvill Press Poetry, 2007; translated by Peter Dale; Canto III, lines 115, 109-110). It is the sign of frantic searches and the significance of key-characters (however, they have their own biography and almost "classic" psychological geography) for the agonizing History of the

World.

Finally, to emphasize the value and implications of Broch's options, I will also mention the decisive role Joyce's novel had for the creations of Ernest Hemingway, and for his entire generation, too: "[...] the influence of his work", confessed Hemingway, "had transformed everything, allowing us to free ourselves from constraints" (*Romanciers aux travail*, Gallimard, 1967, p. 135).

Hermann Broch returns to a motif recurrently encountered in his generation's works: the fate of the empire, its disintegration and decomposition. However, the perspective, compared to that of Robert Musil, is transformed through a much heavier touch on the gear of the military world, on the military hierarchy's myths ongoing a process of dishonoring; on the uniform seen as sign of a mentality or even of a society. All the sacrosanct themes of the time's society - honesty, honor, family, "chastity" - are denounced and scrutinized under the symbol of derision and demystification of the state's supreme "principles". The novel rejects any idea of continuity as regards the conformist respect for the epoch's moral norms, conventions and prejudices. The so-called truths, considered incontestable till then, are questioned or compromised; the reader observes how a *provocative demonic* is established, unmasking the (apparent) tranquility, the hypocrisy and the exhaustion of a society fed by chimeras. "The feelings are lazy" in a world of sleepwalkers, awaken from this devitalized and helpless state: "The crashed happiness of *the crepuscular indolence*, the lost sweetness of the sadness, which conquered his heart and made him shed tears that carried now in their sparkle the eternal lost in the depths" (My emphasis added, Broch, *The Sleepwalkers*). Subjecting himself to self-introspection, Joachim v. Pasenow, the hero of the trilogy's first part, relives feelings and anxieties insinuated by the presence of a devil's emissary (Bertrand), a Mephistopheles destined to an important role: the triggering of the awakening, while playing – fearsome actor – his role so that the revelation of indecisions, the uncertainty and the anxiety would also denote the beginning of the ending of a numb and anachronic society.

Broch's narrator shows his evident preference for the indirect discourse (the indirect free speech) used in the present tense, especially in the first part of the book ("The Romantic"). Commenting and sketching portraits with an extremely dynamic eye, willing to parody by means of thickening the lines, the narrator meditates on the events' development, opening the pathway for digressions or for dissertations following Musil's model (for instance: about the *uniforms* as symbol, he states that "[...] society is segregated between hierarchies and uniforms", or that "actually, this is the true task of the uniform – to demonstrate and to decree the world's order", Ibid.), sliding gradually toward paradox. The usage of various motifs worthy of being commented upon forces, as I have said it, the dissertation about various themes in a certain thematic consonance. The formula is often direct: "After having disserted enough about the advantages of this residential neighborhood, able to prove fitting especially for those used to living in the countryside..." (Ibid.). Hermann Broch's story-teller ability is incontestable in all three parts of the novel; it is also true that in the third part the *song*, inserted between the chapters and the dissertations ("The story of the Berlin girl of the Salvation Army", ibid.), forces an astonishing *collage* and the discourse tends toward a certain detachment or objectivity; to be more exact, it tends to become a type of Brecht-like detachment. As regards the dissertation, the scene is depicted and receives relative autonomy in the narrative space (the mechanism of the village post office; the courier from the Pasenow estate; "the postal bag": "[...] older and more venerable than the modern post, which was established after the stormy 1848", ibid.).

Thus, the novel's alternative structure and the composite development of undeniable originality advance a heterodiegetic novel discourse, as well as essay-type chapters (digressions), such as "The degradation of the values" (a succession of concentrated essays with the same title) and, in conjunction with these, short "stories" from the series "The story of the Berlin girl of the Salvation Army". The third part is scholarly constructed, with the alternated series mentioned above. The impression it gives is that of interlude or of necessary, grave, bitter, ironical comment about events like those in "The Realist". Broch's novel portrays a mature novelist, capable of creating (sometimes) objectified epic constructions, observing destinies and conflicting situations, unforgettable given their narrative developments.

An episode significant for the general visions of the novel's "books" is the funeral of Joachim's brother. Killed in a duel, Helmuth is buried in the cemetery o the Pasenow estate in Stolpin, and the scenes are typical of a novelist with the vocation of the observer and, obviously, of a *narrative view* (the tragic sight is seen through the eyes of Joachim, hence the alternation between the first person and the objectified discourse): "The parents seemed strangely resigned, even the mother. His father greeted him with a handshake and said: / «He fell for honor, for the honor of his name», and he carried on walking up and down the room with heavy and straight steps. Soon after, he said again: / «He fell in the name of honor», and he went out the door. / Joachim had felt the heavy scent of the flowers and garlands, too heavy for a child's casket, a stubborn and absurd thought, and nonetheless, Joachim stopped for a moment in the heavily draped door..." (Ibid.) The parquet pattern, the decorations, the leaves fallen from the garlands next to the casket - the representations thrive in a sequential construction via the juxtaposed organization of the images. "Someone said that the corpse's face had been mutilated by the shot received in full swing. He could barely hear, he remained standing by the casket, put his hand on the lid. And in the embarrassment which takes hold of people when in front of a corpse and of the silence of death, in which everything expands and crashes, everything familiar dissipates and stiffens, branching out, and the air becomes thinner and unbreathable" (Ibid.). This is "the reality fragment" having a multitude and infinitesimal succession of impressions, of sensorial acuity, extended and intensified by the ceremony's atmosphere. The simultaneity effect (and that of juxtaposed collaged cinematographic sequences) is evident also in the narrator's commentary, in the chosen, bizarre even, epithets: the family crypt "gaped jadedly"; Joachim's sensibility ("[...] he then wished for his own death a gentle rainy day, with the sky coming down as if to take with it the soul, which fluidly disperses inside, just like in the arms of Ruzena" (Ibid.). The view associates totally contrasting and "indecent" impressions, explains and, indirectly, sanctions or desecrates (the father and the "he-died-for-honor" *leitmotif*); details remembered apparently illogically and without any justified connections; on their way back to the mansion, Joachim looks at his father and notices: "Between the edging of the black glove and the cuff with the big, black cuff-ling a piece of skin covered by red hair was yet visible." (Ibid.).

Thus, in the first part of the trilogy an ambiguous atmosphere settles in, dominated by the interventions of Bertrand, the demonic conscience of the first part. The novelist draws the portraits according to the rules of Expressionist painting through intensifications and the effect produced by strong contrasts; the family scenes, the old Pasenow and the looks' "frivolity"; the honor (The Iron Cross received by one of the family members in 1813); the superintendent of the Pasenow estate "was not honestly speaking a human being, but a beard"; Berlin, related to Musil's Vienna as regards the street display: military people and civilians – with their distinctive emblems and "signs"; Elisabeth (Joachim's future wife and Bertrand's influence), a character entirely opposing Joachim given her cynicism and radical, non-conformist mentality of opinions. It needs to be said that the characters exist in the parallel mirrors of the other actors on the stage. And beyond these mask-characters or, one could say, puppets in a fair of nothingness, the novelist confirms his seeing and analyzing vocation. The episode of the gradual degradation of the old von Pasenow, of the senile dementia, is absolutely memorable and is reminiscent of the scholarly minuteness of Proust's analysis or the profound look of William Faulkner in *The Sound and the Fury* or, in general, in the cycle initiated with *Sartoris* (as regards the Romanian prose, only Hortensia Papadat-Bengescu has the gift of the clinical analysis, disconcerting through the power of its observation!). The scenes set Joachim's feelings in alternation with the degradation of old Pasenow: the apathy, the confusions, the hallucinatory conditions, the mental messiness. The introspection is created in line with the Freudian formula and is professed when the inner options, the imbalanced conditions need to be determined; namely, it is created in line with the observation of human natures which experience suffering intensified/worsened by the events.

The "sleepwalking" essentially refers to a series of manifestations of several individuals often having strange relations, intensely experiencing anxieties and inner insecurity, not without the longing for a relative stability (balance). The space is more uncertain and even more threatening, being projected as an aggravating factor. Characters devoured by obsessions, by often shameful frustrations, the "interpreters" from *The Sleepwalkers* tend to free themselves from conventions and false principles decreed in society (the obsession excavates from the inside in the case of Joachim, tortured by Bertrand's presence and his far-from-compassionate interventions). Milan Kundera would call "counterpointed coincidence" the association of the demoniac Bertrand to the characters from his 1990 novel *Immortality*: the character Bertrand Bertrand: "But, look, I dozed off again (a sweet, healing sleep takes hold of me each time the name of Bertrand Bertrand is uttered)..." (Milan Kundera, *Nemurirea*, Bucharest, Humanitas, 2002). Broch creates a character with symbolic functions, molding Joachim's life and infiltrating in him the will's anxiety and paralysis, namely, the dependency on this Mephistopheles in various disguises: "And, although they were mean and quarrelsome words, Joachim gladly listened to them because they were a confirmation able to soothe his own suspicions that the demoniac source of all sorrow was in Bertrand. And it even seemed to him like a final overflowing of that Mephistophelian and fully hypocrite influence..." (Broch, *The Sleepwalkers*).

A particular manifestation of the main character from the first part of the trilogy, Joachim, appears to have a Dostoevskyian origin. The conscience of sin and the necessity of penitence conjugate with the more acute and confused sentiment of Bertrand's influence: "Such an ordinary and ugly possibility Joachim didn't take into consideration; Bertrand was indeed a truly loathsome cynic. He suddenly looked at Bertrand: was it possible that this man knew more than he claimed to? Mephistopheles alone could tell the sins for which Margarita had to redeem herself. But Bertrand remained impenetrable. He didn't have any other choice but to submit to Bertrand and to consider his order as another of those trials he had to face" (Ibid.). That "fear network" is thus extended, a prevailing element of the first part's drama, to be found again through intensifications in the second part, dominated by the bizarre conversion of Esch, a truly fascinating Lutheran character given his ambiguous and weird nature.

"The 2 March 1903 has been a bad day for the commercial civil servant August Esch, aged 30" (Ibid.). This is the *incipit* of the second part ("The Anarchist"). Despite the far greater number of characters, some with limited functions, determined by the legitimization of some of Esch's behaviors, the dominant feature of this epic composition is *ugliness*, a spectacle of generalized degradation, of mutilation and inner disorder. The ugliness, having multiple connections with the sordid and the promiscuous, creates the narrative space for a chronotope where the narrative dissertation on life and death, on a *ruined time*, on the sleep of a world incapable of noticing the somber and apocalyptical signs of the future, is set under the emblem of a gradually constructed tragic. The erotic too is stained by the sordid (the relation Esch – Erna, the sister of the customs officer Balthasar Korn from Mannheim or the relation between "mother" Hentjen and Esch, concluded with a strange marriage, based on a desperate attraction of the senses).

Actually, the book is dominated by the presence of August Esch, a character who expresses the frustrations and unsettled fury of a lost world, lacking the trust in the long ago compromised and de-sanctified values of the beginning of the XX century. The novel's entire universe is influenced, up to a point, by this character originating in Dostoevsky's world; he has – keeping the proportions and taking into account the biography, formation and destiny of Dostoevsky's characters – common features with Stavroghin from *The Demons* (given his versatile nature, willing to carry out any compromises or crimes), with Svidrigad'lov from *Crime and Punishment* (his demonism and cynicism, his rejection of any moral principle) and, to a certain extent, with Kirilov from *The Possessed*, who was searching for the existence of God, but of a vague, essentially contested God. Esch himself is an anxious character, feeding an eternal fury, a dissatisfaction metamorphosed in obsession. The blind and anarchical fury is the fury of one of Kafka's employees: "[...] the fury against an organization that, under the guise of a beautiful order, of smooth and shiny corridors, of ordered records hides all possible outrages. And this is what they call stability! One is either a prosecutor or a president [...]. He mostly wanted to go downstairs in the offices of the accountancy department, to tell those blind people there that they should tear themselves from the prison of numbers and columns of deceiving numbers and to free themselves, the way he had done it without second thoughts, yes, this is what they should all do, even with the risk of, just like him and together with him, having to emigrate later on to America" (Ibid.). The idea that *anarchy* "ruled everywhere in the world" is the constant preoccupation of Esch, himself in a furious and always agitated search for revenge against what he thought was an anarchic and dangerous society. Hence, the continuously inflamed hatred against Bertrand, seen as an embodiment of Evil, of sin.

Despite the inner nature of Dostoevsky's heroes and despite their convictions, the confusion of values, the fanaticism and the obstinacy for certain ideas also characterize the very complex and nuanced hero created by Broch. The rebellion and the search for a meaning, in disorder and total drifting; the opposition to that which he considers anarchy and evil are typical of a primitive, and therefore more dangerous, fanatic: "[...] no, order was being established in this world not according to the people, good or bad, but according to certain forces, we don't know whether good or bad" (Ibid.); in line with Esch's opinion, this is a world where crime and punishment, or the deviation from moral norms have entered an extremely harmful regime of disorder: "Nothing was graspable anymore, with only one clear meaning! [...] And given the way Esch thought with the greatest hatred of the surrounding world and of the pigs that deserved to be slaughtered, the way it was actually fitting to do with pigs, he ended up hating more clearly and more strongly president Bertrand, he hated him both for his vices and for his crimes. He tried to imagine him how, in his upper class world, with a thick cigar in his hand, he sat on his upholstered furniture, in his castle, and when this image full of distinction seemed to him as if finally lifting up from a cloud of smoke, it looked like the image of a chubby tailor, very similar to the portrait of mister Hentjen, which hanged in the restaurant above the sideboard". (Ibid.)

The impressions, the perception and the correspondences belong to a character created in the spirit and with the means of an expressionist representation; the deformation of the lines, the multiplication or the allocation within a composition full of contrasts and unexpected associations develop from the eye of the expressionist image. We say that the *ugliness* (which it can be found in the expressionist graphics or painting) stimulates and provokes that inner *disorder* – drifting and fear, desperate cry and confusion, so favorable to the "sleepwalking" of the depicted World, where is written the journey of this character symptomatic for a world which is living, still latently, its future ending. "Things are more than close, and more than distant, things are like a naïve child, and the traveler who went on the train and who longs from afar for his wife or maybe just for his homeland and his native environment, is like someone whose sight is starting to fade away and who is invaded by a mild fear that he could go blind. Many things became distorted around him, at least this is what he tells himself, as soon as he covered his face with his coat, and nevertheless, inside him starts to sprout a science which he had until then ignored. *He is on the verge of entering sleepwalking.*" (My emphasis added, ibid.). The analysis forces a special attention for the details and a perfect suitability to the interchanges and inner swings of the character. However, the second part uses not only a very fine and subtle psychoanalytical instrument, but also a format created with the digressive "surfaces" of the fundamental motifs: the monstrous and the ugliness, the tragic confusion of a world still unable to understand and to lucidly assume its punishment.

***

The ambiguity affects the represented worlds and the novel's fictive universe perceives the merge real-unreal, the dissociations being rather difficult to make. In a world where – prophetically – the downfall seems to be prepared by murder (World War I), the destinies live under the empire of grave, crashing events. As regards the structures, I have already asserted that the third part, "The Realist", employs a diversified discourse through digressions and through songs, actually genuine choir fragments, lyrically commenting the inevitable degradation process. Given their compositional interchange, what else could the concentrated essays with a definite reflexive character from the series "The Degradation of the Values" be?

The moment with repercussions for the history of the times is the deplorable ending of World War I. In numerous scenes are registered the signs – from the points of view of the outraged and/or the mentally destroyed beings – of the calamity announced by Thomas Mann in *The Magic Mountain* (Hans Castorp leaves the asylum loosing his trail in the war's chaos).

The Sleepwalkers does not depict genuine war scenes. In 1920, Ernst Jünger wrote in *The Storm of Steel* probably the most dramatic confession about the bloody sight of the trenches. And in 1919, *Wooden Crosses*, the novel by Roland Dorgelès, was published. In 1929, two books in which the individual drama is projected on the background of the conflict were published: *All Quiet on the Western Front* by Erich Maria Remarque and *A Farewell to Arms* by Ernest Hemingway. A phenomenon was taking place in the creative space and in that of transcending reality in and through fiction. In Romania, it was analyzed by Eugen Lovinescu and then it did not take long for the works to appear, from the general epos of a collective drama: *Balaurul* ("The Dragon") by Hortensia Papadat-Bengescu; *Întunecare* ("Darkening") by Cezar Petrescu; a truly remarkable and often ignored book is *1916*, the novel by Felix Aderca; *Pădurea Spânzuraților* ("The Forest of the Hanged"), the epic drama by Liviu Rebreanu, work of an extraordinary psychological tension, and *Ultima noapte de dragoste, întâia noapte de război* ("The Last Night of Love, the First Night of War") where Camil Petrescu constructs the novel's second part in the already acknowledged formula of the authenticity prose.

The third book of Broch's trilogy does not weaken the grave images of the war: a military hospital, a space of desperation and individual degradation, a territory of suffering and agony. The most relevant aspects of the third part are revealed on two relatively distinct narrative levels. For the configuration of the three parts' fundamental meanings, the main axis of the novel is realized by the meeting between Pasenow, now military commander in a border town, and Esch, editor and publisher of the newspaper *Kurtrierscher Bote*, a mix between a mystic, religious fanatic and a pastor "illuminated" by a faith which seemed to have originated in the rigor of Luther's protest.

In this indefinite space, the emergence of the strange Wilhelm Huguenau – "whose forerunners", as testifies the narrator tempted to (partially) recreate a suspicious biography, "had probably borne the name Hagenau before Alsace was occupied in 1682 by the troops of Condé" (Broch, *The Sleepwalkers*) -, produces radical changes of perspective and simultaneously gives a different vision, with "infiltrations" of grotesque, picaresque and dark, bitter irony, of a desperate world after the failure of a war that claimed millions of lives! The first sentences of the third part create the portrait – conjugated with the data of a classic biography – of this war's "product", of the simulations and of the lies, the forging of his own biography (Huguenau is a deserter and the information given by the narrator in the acknowledged formula of heterodiegetic narrative is suggestive for the disintegration process of the German society, demystified and thus, analyzed with the aim of revealing its numb joints). Because, as the future deserter notices, "the world stretches like in a glass cage – Huguenau unwillingly thought of one of those cages in which cheese is kept –, *the world was ashy, wormy and totally dead*, in that silence unbroken by anything" (My emphasis added, ibid.). It feels like reading Ernst Jünger and rediscovering accents from the *Paris Diaries*, with that bitter taste of the collapse, of the inevitable and undeniable forthcoming of the apocalypse of a new defeat, this time at the end of World War II. "*The world was ashy*" is actually the motif of this book populated by sleepwalkers, by disjointed, demoralized and defeated beings. Therefore, the show offered by Huguenau, with the construction of lies and the improvised biography, is even more grotesque and it insinuates the lamentable ending of a world standing no chance, lacking anything heroic or generous.

The "sleepwalking" could also mean an alternative for the human being who remained a prisoner to the state, to the system, to the war. A deserter and now a merchant who improvises businesses, relations etc, Huguenau is saved by the sleepwalking of the first steps he took by leaving the military: "But this does not explain the fact that Huguenau had managed to escape in one piece from Belgium [where his German military unit was stationed]; to a larger extent, it could have been explained by *the certainty of a true sleepwalker*, which he had exercised in that dangerous zone; he used to walk around in the fresh air of early spring, as under a glass of indifference, thus, separating himself from the surrounding world, while still living in it..." (My emphasis added, ibid.). As I have stated before, the novel develops on various levels and the narrative levels are justified by parallel events as well. In a small town in the Mosele valley, in the military hospital, history reveals its most somber and grave face: the mason Ludwig Gödicke is brought back to life as a crashed being, terrifyingly mutilated; a young lieutenant, Jaretzki, with an amputated arm, has the revelation of desperation together with the military doctors (Kuhlenbeck, Flurschütz); they live haunted by the infernal scenes of the war still going on a few kilometers away from town; cynicism and skepticism take the place of the enthusiasm felt during the first years of fighting. We find ourselves before the ending, if there truly is a possible ending: "Jaretzki said: / «The future war? You don't actually believe that this one will ever end?»". For the time being, the war belongs to the surgeons, and that cursed image of the war is still present: "«Tell me, Jaretzki, do you understand that we quietly walk around this place, that life goes on quietly, while just a few kilometers away from us *people hack each other with enthusiasm*?»" (My emphasis added, ibid.).

Because *The Sleepwalkers*, just like the novels mentioned before – although Broch's work has a stronger, graver and at the same time a more skeptical inner drama -, demystifies the erotic traditions of Prussian patriotism and invincibility. It is maybe the warning of one of the great consciences of German culture, a warning heard in those years (1931-1932) when the Nazis were consolidating doctrinairely and noisily their future insanity: the other world war would follow, not ignored by the novelist's lucid heroes. The former mason restored to life in the military hospital is invited by the narrator to announce it: "Gödicke was pointing with both his crutches to the flames on the other side and was enthusiastically shouting: / «Doomsday... resurrected... who is not resurrected goes straight to hell... you all go to hell... all... right now...»" (Ibid.).

The sleepwalking allows some people to live in this age of upheavals and re-evaluations of all truths accepted before without judgment: in the absence of tragic confrontations like that of the war and of the degradation of all human relations. A character of great inner tension, surveyed psychoanalytically, is Hanna Wendling, the wife of the jurist Heinrich Wendling who lived somewhere in Romania at the time of the war. The life of the lonely wife was, as the narrator (a careful observer of sad lucidity) registers, "a life largely emptied by any substance and maybe therefore lacking importance" (Ibid.). She is one of the individuals on whom the events take action gradually, insinuatingly, devitalizingly, annulling her femininity and the joy of the flesh, forbidden, postponed until a serious alienation: "[...] the weird feeling of estrangement, an estrangement which could no longer be denied" (Ibid.). The analytical discourse metamorphoses slowly in the clinic "file" of a disease contaminating an interrelated world, subjected to the same process of inner decline. Within the formula of introspection and self-referentiality, the destiny of Hanna Wendling is examined using an anamnesis exempted from the established details: "the borderline between *lucidity* and *vertigo* is not always easy to maintain and, if the Russian love of people was firstly defined as vertigo or if it were used as the name of the normal social relationship between people or even if the general insight of things needs to be taken as vertigo or lucidity, this at last remains undecided. Nevertheless, it is impossible for lucidity to have a *feeling of entropy* or an absolute zero, an absolute zero toward which all relations restlessly tend with necessity. [...] people's entropy is their own *absolute estrangement*, and that which man had named before as harmony or balance was probably just a model, a model which the man made up and had to make up from social structures, as long as he was a part of it. However, the more estranged he becomes, the more degraded and isolated the things around him become ..." (My emphasis added, ibid.).

Finally, the narrative level conceived as the development of certain characters from the first two parts, Pasenow and Esch, inflects (apparently according to the narrative strategies "of disorientation") Esch's evolution, a blend of abjection and fanaticism, of continuous rage, proclaiming an improvised pastor, an associate of Huguenau, a grotesque and at the same time ridiculous Don Quixote: "[...] but who here and in these conditions has to become the occasion for a necessary and inevitable fight between authorities and justice, *for a fight between two unrealities*, between two restraining acts, a fight to always take place just like the crusade of Don Quixote against a world which does not want to match up with the claims of the spirit's longing for order" (My emphasis added, ibid.). The theoretic, essayistic excursus, more recurrent and fuller of warnings, is included in *the series of essays* "The degradation of values". The insertion of the texts in the novel's composition is legitimized in the third part by the collection of events and phenomena emerging from the spectacle of these successive downfalls, sufferings and surrenders of the individual assaulted and conquered by loneliness. The revelation of suffering and failure is omnipresent in the microcosm of the German town where major Pasenow confronts his desperate loneliness, his amnesias and his memory's volutes. One of the doctors that Pasenow met will say that: "[...] *the entire world is a prison...* anyway, it won't last long... moreover, this ramshackle should have been long ago evacuated..." (My emphasis added, ibid.). He apparently refers to the evacuation of the hospital, but the doctor's voice proclaims an ending of a few *dead souls*.

A motif of the third part, the loneliness/alienation is repeated from the perspective of the reflexive, essayistic discourse, as well as from the perspective of the choir's comments, expressed in the tenth "Story of the Berlin girl of the Salvation Army": "I had now, so it seemed, two beings in my hand, and still I don't know anything about them, I don't know what they think and what they will have for dinner; man is so lonely, that no one, not even God who anyway created man, knows anything about him!" (Ibid.).

Occasionally, Hermann Broch claims one of his sources, a fundamental model of the literature of German expression, even though Kafka's work does not seem to have been mentioned by him. However, one can distinguish Kafka's vision in the first essay of the cycle "The degradation of values", as a comment on the discourse of the author of *The Process* and *The Castle*: "The unreal is the illogic. And our age seems unable to overcome the climax of the illogic, of the anti-logic; it is as if the monstrous reality of the war suspended the reality of the world. The fantastic becomes logical reality." (Ibid.). Written when Musil was constructing his amazing masterpiece, unfinished just like the always threatened and more acutely tragic World, Broch's book is dedicated to the fantastic of an apocalyptic and "tragic infra-reality".

The resources of the anti-novel

"*La question du style, c'est toujours l'examen, le pesant d'un object pointu. Parfois seulement d'une pleume. Mais aussi bien d'un stylet, voire d'un poignard. A l'aide desquels on peut, certes, attaquer cruellement ce à quoi la philosophie en appelle sous le nom de matière ou de matrice, pour y enfoncer une marque, y laisser une empreinte ou une forme, mais aussi pour repousser une forme menaçante, la tenir à distance, la refouler, s'en garder – se pliant alors ou repliant, en fuite, derrière des voiles*" (Jacques Derrida, *Spurs: Nietzsche's Styles/Éperons: Les Styles de Nietzsche*, The University of Chicago Press, Chicago and London, 1978; p. 36).

I am sure that in Derrida's text there are the expressive and extremely meaningful characteristics of the prose open to the word, to the free play of the illogic and of unreality, provoked and instigated by another perspective on the World, on human relations and on a tired logic, exhausted by ordinary affirmations, truisms and sleep-compelling conventions. Like a stiletto, having the force and fierceness of a dagger, the narrative discourse of the prose of Witold Gombrowicz inaugurates a form of literature in order to actually reiterate older experiences, reigned by one of the world's great novelists: Rabelais.

In fact, regarding Gombrowicz, a similar process of opacity or, to be more exact, of blindness is reedited just like in the case of Kafka. The recognition will come later on, although – as it is often noted in literary or narrative histories – the Polish novelist anticipates the experience of Sartre and, in general, he anticipates the theatre of the absurd (except for Eugen Ionescu and the first prose pieces of the Romanian writer Eugen Urmuz published in 1922), the transformations of the prose decided to unsettle the structures and conventions of classic realism, the logic of the narrative where no surprises can intervene. Suggestive is the fact that, especially after the publishing of the *Journal* (1953), the European literary critics and later the Polish critics as well salute his new and modern spirit, the writer's natural inclination for the deconstruction of all assertions, of the "truths" kept, due to inertia and immobility, in the thought and the evaluation of the severed realities of an existence rendered common by the ordinary affirmations and truisms of some subsequent generations educated in the school of conformism and of comfortable obedience.

Once it was recognized or at least noticed by a few critics receptive to the formula adopted by the Polish writer, his novel *Ferdydurke* (1937) was compared to the works of Jean-Paul Sartre and especially to *Nausea*, novel published one year after the ignored book by Gombrowicz.

Beyond the questionable hierarchies of literary history or of the (interested) critics, the novel published in Poland two years before the start of the Polish tragedy, rediscovered the taste for crude humor, for irony and for parody-play, decomposing the logic relations and the order established through the re-examination *in absurd* of the human being, of its inner mechanisms, restoring a new thinking order about institutions, about men's dependence on them, the anachronism and the conformism - apparently incurable flaws of the society unable to notice the serious signs of the future. The psychologism, the predictable narrative situations, the melodramatic, the "nostalgia" of a Poland still inhabited by *szlachta*[1], with mansions belonging to old and powerless noble families; the education system; the enormousness of some aberrations of the regime established at that time etc., they all are material for derision and ridicule. Maxime Herman, the author of a (massive) literary history of the Polish literature, asserted that the main problem of the novel *Ferdydurke* was infantilism, the "immaturity" as response to certain situations - as one could draw from the vague comments of the French researcher (cf. M. Herman, *Histoire de la Littérature polonaise* (Des origins

[1] The Polish term *szlachta* designates the nobility class that arose in Poland during the Middle Ages and lasted until the XIX century (Translator's note).

à 1961), Paris, A. G. Nizet éditeur, 1963; p. 569). To a certain extent, the childhood and the adolescence are opposed to society's dead seas. However, the grotesque and the satirical virulence are far more important in the novel and together with the analysis of several institutions, as I have already mentioned, represent the dominant features of the novel.

Gombrowicz's *Journal* is able to explain far more convincingly the nature of the book; it is obvious that *Ferdydurke* does not intent to be anything but an intolerant and destructive, nonconformist and iconoclast discourse. Nothing escapes the book's violent comments aimed to parody: the family, the school, the boyars, the childhood, the noisy patriotism, the evidently false rhetoric about homeland, tradition etc. It is some sort of a *settling account* with a world that used to exist; with a Poland "which was created by its historical conditions and its position in the world (in other words, with a weak Poland)" (Witold Gombrowicz, *Trans-Atlantic*, Bucharest, Univers, 1999). The recourse to childhood and the placement of the child at the centre of this aggressive analysis ratifies in fact another statement from the author's *Preface* to *Trans-Atlantic*: "Is there something in it about Poland? But I have never written a word about anything else but myself" (Gombrowicz, 1999). Namely, in the writer's biography the events are projected as direct, individual experience, transfigured in the text; Gombrowicz arrived in Buenos Aires in 1939, and he will live there until 1963! Gombrowicz owes the recognition of his works' translations and the publishing of the originals to France. Only from this moment onward, his work will enter the course and the value judgment aimed at rehabilitating or making a writer better known, a forerunner of experiences encountered in Beckett's work or in the works of writers formed in the school of existentialism and especially of the absurd.

Undoubtedly, Milan Kundera is right when he underlines the supremacy of Gombrowicz's work in relation with Sartre's *Nausea*: "[...] an unknown Gombrowicz", writes Kundera in *Testaments Betrayed*, "a famous Sartre, in that case, to say it like this, *Nausea* confiscated, in the history of the novel, the place owed to Gombrowicz" (Kundera, 1993); the idea that the novel *Fer-*

dydurke recovers, as I have said it above, another journey of the genre, starting with Rabelais and continuing with the great novel of the XVIII century (Fielding and Sterne) is thoroughly confirmed by the novels' heterogeneous nature, by their openness to protean dimensions, in which the tragic and the comic, the grotesque and the mask (continuously transforming themselves) define a protean structure, eclectic like the vision greedy for the always renewed movements of the world, on that programmed "disorder" (entropy) of space and time in a chronotope permeable to the unexpected mutations of the real and surreal.

There are a few novel *forms* (the term "forms" denotes in this case more than the accepted or new invariants of the genre, revealing innovations regarding various combinatory elements, regarding the play and the parody) which have potential connections with Musil's and Broch's narrative. I believe that the most important element is the incisive and always stinging irony and the digression too, where the commentary, the monologue reflection, the connections and the intertextuality lack any limitations, and are free to merge and conjugate. This is, in Kundera's words, "the third age of the novel", of its history. If I were to determine an analogy, primarily valid for the "classic" realist novel (Balzac), an analogy regarding the signifier and the transgression through literature of a reality *in nuce*, I would quote a fragment from one of Oscar Wilde's essays, *The Unleashing of the Lie*. For the author of *The Portrait of Dorian Gray*, the model was the narrative cycle of Balzac; to quote: "Schopenhauer has analysed the pessimism that characterises modern thought, but Hamlet invented it. [...] Literature always anticipates life. It does not copy it, but moulds it to its purpose. The nineteenth century, as we know it, is largely an invention of Balzac. Our Luciens de Rubempre, our Rastignacs, and De Marsays made their first appearance on the stage of the *Comédie Humaine*. We are merely carrying out, with footnotes and unnecessary additions, the whim or fancy or creative vision of a great novelist." (Oscar Wilde, *The Decay of Lying: An Observation*[2]). In fact, the great novel-

[2] Oscar Wilde, *The Decay of Lying: An Observation*, available at www.readbookonline.net.

ists re-establish and ratify the existential quivers and give them a revealing ontological and cognitive dimension; this is a defining process for the creative act and for the auto-telic regime of discoveries and of the proper communication.

In the *Preface* to *Trans-Atlantic*, Gombrowicz explains in *explicit poetics* the nature of the discourse where the narrator and the character are Gombrowicz, a name separated from the author, transformed in an extremely free auctorial narrator, having an often confusing mobility; hence, the need to explain and to avoid the superficial or limited reading. Around the publishing date in Poland (1953), the writer is therefore forced to entail "a more profound and complex reading of the text" (Gombrowicz, 1999). The novelist does not hide the pride of a new epic experience: "I am one of those ambitious hunters who, if they miss, they miss only when they point to a bigger game" (Ibid.). The introductory text is equally a prologue for the reader facing the novel *Ferdydurke*. The satire of a Poland petrified in its admiration for its history; the historical context (in 1937 and then 1953) and the geo-political aspects of Poland need *revisions*! They are therefore valid for the narrative discourse as well, other than the traditional one and – it appears to the Polish novelist – inadequate for another examination (revision!) of the consciences, textbooks, the deformed communication found in schools, in the life of various social categories of the old and – now – anachronic Poland. It is the heresy of the writer; he assumes it by writing a "story": "It is but a story, nothing more that a *narrated world*, which can have value only if it proves to be *funny, colorful, revealing* and *stimulating*" (My emphasis added, ibid.).

The 1937 novel questions some of literature's fundamental themes; the borderline between seriousness and bantering irony, the "caricatured" time or simply, the demystification of certain motifs which enforce themselves on the warned reader. The narrative self, a speculative self, registers: "It was the *dread* of nonexistence, the *terror* of extinction, it was the *angst* of nonlife, the *fear* of unreality, a biological scream of all my cells in the face of an inner disintegration when all would be blown to pieces and scattered to the winds. It was the *fear* of unseemly pettiness and mediocrity, the *fright* of distraction, [...], the *dread* of rape [...] there was something [...] that I would call a sense of inner, intermolecular mockery and derision" (Witold Gombrowicz, *Ferdydurke*, Yale University Press / New Haven & London, 2000; my emphasis added, pp. 1-2). The discourse maintains, at least throughout the first ten chapters (the titles are obviously a parody and they replicate, in their form, the titles of the XVIII century novels), the appearance of the first-person novel, with an evident emphasis on the oral, on the first person's digressive mobility. It alternates, in serious register and in ironic, allusive expression, the meditation and the narration using forms apparently belonging to the 1940s novel. The bellowed reflection, revolted like in a burning pamphlet, is recurrent in the novel preparing, announcing or opening at the end of narrated situations through the participation of the directly involved narrative self: "Oh, those judgments, the bottomless pit of people's judgments and opinions about your wisdom", "I mean the opinions of those other aunts - the cultural aunts, those female semi-writers and tacked-on semi-critics who make pronouncements in literary magazines." (Gombrowicz, 2000, p. 6).

However, the rhetoric discharged against the questionable "authorities" in culture, sometimes recalling Eugen Ionescu's theatre and – beyond the historical moment and the reasoning and motivation of the monologued discourse – the "German trilogy" of Louis-Ferdinand Céline, has the cruelty and incurable, violent line of argument; the interrogation and the exclamation are part of the rhetoric props of this monologue interrupted occasionally by the charged and likewise parodied situations: "Or is it because I've lived in an era that, every five minutes, emits new fads and slogans, and at the slightest opportunity, grimaces convulsively - a transitory era?..." (Ibid., p. 11).

The game of simulations presides over the epic construction of a novel displaying an ostentatious title lacking a definite meaning: "Ferdydurke". Chapter I, "Abduction", starts (I have quoted a few passages above) with the confession of a rebel against conventions, human relations, false hierarchies, contesting and arguing with "the semi-educated rabble" (Ibid., p. 8), to later on introduce the concept of *the form*. Gombrowicz examines, formulating a concept with a meaning larger than the literary theoretician could understand; in reality, a program, aware of its being a new experience, until then unprecedented in narrative history. Maybe that is why it maintains, through the simulating mechanism, the appearances of the "traditional" novel: "[...] I begin, amid shimmering and finely chiseled forms, to write the first pages of my very own *oeuvre*, which will be just like me, identical with me, the sum total of me, an *oeuvre* in which I will be free to expound my own views against everything and everyone (Ibid., p. 14).

The narrator campaigns against stupidity ("it occurred to me that I had become some kind of mystical conjurer of stupidity", ibid., p. 25), acutely being revolted by the grotesque and "ugliness". The battle is carried against the convention, the sufficiency, the deformed and stupid-making display of the institutions, among which the epoch's education system looked like the field with the most harmful consequences: "It is in the prime youth that man sinks into empty phrases and the grimaces. It's in this smithy that our maturity is forged." (Ibid., p. 68). The play of the imaginary and of the conventions' unraveling extends through the intervention of a narrator who is far from humble and has no complexes; the *alter ego* of the narrator enters this performance and broadens it decomposing the accredited representations, transgressing the lines of the verisimilar and of realist veracity; a vague parody frees itself from the constraints typical of the traditional or psychologising novel; nothing from such models is left out of the iconoclast discourse of the novelist tempted to place under the sign of derision the ridiculous prides of the *szlachta*, their diminished or even counterfeited history, while adolescence too (the pharisaic innocence) is demystified. The demystification continues and is always stimulated by the pleasure of unmasking all the questionable values.

Thus, in this regard, the quote from the essay of Jacques Derrida is totally legitimate given the technique and the rhetoric of the novelist: he deconstructs while simultaneously disclosing the narrative mechanisms and the text, developing the discourse based on a syntax willingly complicated by the author. His proclaimed *poetics* undeniably announces future experiences in the European literatures of the 1940s to the 1960s: "[...] and there is the expert thoroughly studying the author's material, whereupon the masterpiece goes out into the world and to the reader, and what was conceived in utter and absolute agony is now received piecemeal, between a telephone call and a hamburger. Here is the writer who with all his heart and soul, with his art, in anguish and travail offers nourishment – there is the reader who'll have none of it, and if he wants it, it's only in passing, offhandedly, until the phone rings. [...] Doesn't all form rely on the process of exclusion, isn't all construction a process of whittling down, can a word express anything but a part of reality? The rest is silence. And finally, do we create form or does form create us? We think we are the ones who construct it, but that's an illusion, because we are, in equal measure, constructed by the construction." (Ibid., p. 72).

The compromising of the old poetics and accepted assertions about the novel's structure and/or about the text's poetics, the problem of the creator and of the "active" form etc. justify the parody and the non-conformist nature of the work; the short-story included in the text, which seems to copy the model of Cervantes or of the XVIII century novel - *Filidor* (chapters V and XI: "The Child Runs Deep in Filidor" and "The Child Runs Deep in Filibert") appears to contradict any traditional model and to certify the deconstruction of previous forms found in Polish literature; the short-story "[...] is a construction in reverse, a passage or, strictly speaking, a coda, it's a trill, or rather a twist, a twisting of the gut" (Ibid., p. 69). The parody mechanism is exercised virtuously with endless subjacent connections and it is deliberately compromised; the banter and the derision continue to enrich the disguise or, in effect, the book's infinite *carnivalesque.*

Un-dissimulated, the book's meaning seems to be expressed polemically in the style of the avant-garde manifestoes: "And – it's possible – that the motive and goal for writing this book is solely show these gentlemen my disdain for them, to agitate, irritate, and enrage them, and to get them out of my way." (Ibid.,

p. 197). Otherwise, the play on creation, masterpiece and artist continues with other comments enclosed in the same type of acclaimed, ostentatious monologue which seems to call out for a duel in the name of an art cleansed and detached from all the official models proclaimed as such in school – common places for the usage of those willing to accept them. The dispute continues: "It is in the prime youth that man sinks into empty phrases and the grimaces. It's in this smithy that our maturity is forged." (Ibid., p. 68). *On "the ridicule of friction"* could be defined as the vast digression written in the same provoking, determined, utterly irreverent stile. The creator ("for fifty years") has been working on the future masterpiece (I have already quoted the passage on construction). But beyond the exposed, caricatured mechanism set in absurd connections, the play will continue through the widening of the irony and of the enormous, through simulation and successive dissimulating acts: "These are then the basic fundamental and philosophical reasons that have induced me to build a work on a foundation of individual parts – treating the work itself as a particle of the work, man as a union of parts, and mankind as a composite of parts and pieces." (Ibid., p. 74)

The detachment is categorical even in this polemic play in which the parodied element (the work's traditional canons) discovers through the mobility of a new logic (of the absurd) a parodying and later a direct discourse: "And so help me God – I don't hesitate to admit it – I don't want to have anything to do with your Art, gentlemen, which I can't stand, just as mush as I don't want to have anything to do with you... because I can't stand you, with your ideas, your artistic posturing, and all that artistic little world of yours." (Idem) Apart from the conventions of this type of direct discourse suitable to the most percussive rhetoric, the tone becomes more violent and aggressive when it refers to the exponents of the official, endorsed literature: "For shame, gentlemen, for shame, shame and shame again! I'm not a philosopher and theoretician, no – but I'm talking about you, I'm talking about your life, do understand me, I'm purely and simply troubled by your personal situation." (Ibid., pp. 76-77) The voice of the auctorial narrator is ever stronger, the imprecations come one after the other, and the smeared "poetic art" of those who were or still are resembles the agitated, frustrated, irritated and ever more passionate discourse of Céline from the novels of the "German trilogy". Undoubtedly, no connection can be made as regards the time and the *pro domo* dissertation of the French novelist, who was kept in the memory of literary history only thanks to his narrative genius and not due to the serious mistakes made in the years preceding and during World War II. The distance between the real dissertation and the parody, between the aesthetic program open to the anti-novel and the intentionally over-dimensioned struggle can be of course determined. Important is the fact that Witold Gombrowicz introduces in the European prose the experience of the absurd, of a polemic novel engaged in the battle against the exhausted and devitalized forms, strangled by the tricks (the psychological novel, the historic novel, the melodramatic novel etc.), continuing – polemic also due to the parody's mechanisms – that which Robert Musil or Hermann Broch had already realized.

The Polish writer reinstated the *problem-novel*, the open forms of the genre, to sort of remind us about the forerunners of the carnivalesque novel where the burlesque, the grotesque mask, the play and its instances receive the supremacy needed for a renewal of the narrative structures. From now onwards, the two "models", Filidor and Filibert", free the play, the paradoxes and the adventure of the words destined to a wide and loud polemic dedicated first of all to art: "Oh, the power of Form! Nations die because of it. It is the cause of wars. It creates something in us that is not of us. If you make light of it you'll never understand stupidity nor evil nor crime. It governs our slightest impulses." (Ibid., p. 80) The reproaches are far more numerous and the revolt converts into mockery or banter.

Moreover, within the continuous movement between the area of the real and of the un-real or of the non-real: "[...] no one knows anymore what is real and what doesn't even exist, what is truth and what is illusion, what one feels or doesn't feel, what is natural behavior and what is affectation or make-believe, and, what *should be* becomes confused with what inexorably *is*, one disqualifying the other, one depriving the other of all *raison d'etre*, oh, what a great schooling in unreality." (Ibid., p. 131) The chapters have titles generated by the same taste for farce and parody emphasizing the polemic "un-seriousness" of the book constantly tempted to mine forms and mentalities, human relations and institutions; the fragmentariness, the effect of a continuum of the phrases' syntax, the collage elements etc. (chapter IX "Peeping and Further Incursion into Modernity"). A "formula of the disgust" triggers more and more comments, apparently disorganized references, generating thus an image of surrealist panorama: the Vichy pills, the rubber device for female exercise, Chaplin's memoirs, with the recollection of H. G. Wells (and "the dance of his own invention", p. 155); everything becomes an utopia, associating – absurdly – utterly unusual interiors and referents: "The schoolgirl actually slept in public, not in private, she had no private life at night, and this hard public life united her with Europe, America, with Hitler, Mussolini, and Stalin, with labor camps, flag waving, hotels, railroad stations, giving her an immensely wide scope, eliminating the need for a room of her own. Her bedsheets, stashed in the hideaway sofa, had an auxiliary character, they could at most be an accessory to sleep." (Ibid., pp. 155-156) It is comparable to the works of Urmuz or the dialogues of Ionescu's theatre; it recalls the same non-conformism against the philistines and against the ugly spirit of a world prepared to die as well.

The farce and the open props of derision do not however lack a certain meaning; it is actually a false accusation, accomplished via the play of the double meaning and of the ambiguous; otherwise, the questions are indeed serious and they hide the deep dissatisfaction of the writer involved in the narrative play: "And the face of this century – the face of the twentieth century, the century of all centuries gone mad, lurked ambiguously like Silenus in the thicket." (Ibid., p. 158) Nothing can stop the avalanche of words, of provocative and even aggressive combinations, bantering continuously and denouncing the truisms and the clichés: "[...] she read them for the sake of the poet's loneliness, the poet's work, the poet's mission, the poet's role, the poet's suffering, the poet's originality, the poet's calling, and even for the sake of the poet's soul." (Ibid., p. 160) The phrase builds up through repetition and compromises the word, the used rhetoric. By disarticulating and decomposing, the sentence looses its original meaning, undoing thus the automatisms and the routine of the thought: "Wasn't this why Trocki tortured? Or Torquemada? What was the nature of Torquemada's schoolgirl? Quietly, quietly." (Ibid., p. 157)

The second level of the novel, the encounter with the countryside and the anachronic territory of the rural nobility, has the savor and the humor of satirical prose. The carnivalesque presides here too, over the view of the narrator returned in a world not mystified at all. On the contrary, the display is polemic here as well, denouncing and demystifying a universe frequently glorified by the tradition of the *szlachta* and of the relations with the peasants; the patriarchal-like literature, the idealization of the past and the eulogy of the countryside are sanctioned according to the same manner of responding; the irony and the acid, sarcastic and cruel outlook, the discourse based on accumulation and registering of certain heteroclite elements have the effects desired by the narrator: "And just as he finished saying these words a breeze blew gently on our chicks, there were no more houses, streets, gutters, sewers, hairdressers, windows, workers, wives, mothers and daughters, vermin, cabbage, stuffy air, cramped spaces, dust, proprietors, artisans, shoes, blouses, hats, heels, streetcars, shops, vegetables, smart alecks, shop signs, blackheads, stuff, glances, hair, eyebrows, lips, sidewalks, bellies, tools, organs, hiccups, knees, elbows, windowpanes, shouts, sniveling, spitting, throat clearing, conversations, children, clatter. We came to the city limits. Ahead of us – fields, forests." (Ibid., pp. 206-207) Beyond the "border", a desolate expanse begins; the world metamorphoses in grotesque, in some kind of a nightmare of emptiness and ugliness: "This was the first time I had ever observed a whole village hurriedly transforming itself into dogs on the strength of the law of mimicry and out of fear of humanization, too intensely applied." (Ibid., p. 210)

The return to childhood memories, to a different time – the time of recollection, becomes impossible in a context dominated by the views of the degradation and of the nothingness. *Ferdydurke* announces thus a grave literature which is not prone to compromises and is aroused by history, by the unstable destiny of the individual attacked by threats, by the roars of the unleashed animals. Literature discovers another face, recalling other predecessors: skeptics, deceived and betrayed, answering via the carnivalesque or absurd enormity belonging to things and to people. Witold Gombrowicz does not hide his own poetics and communicates it keeping a hidden, sad smile: "One would also need to establish, proclaim, and define whether the work is a novel, a memoir, a parody, a lampoon, a variation on a fantasy, or a study of some kind – and what prevails in it: humor, irony, or some deeper meaning, sarcasm, persiflage, invective, rubbish, *pur nonsense*, *pur claptrapism*, and more, whether it's simply a pose, pretense, make-believe, bunkum, artificiality, paucity of wit, anemia of emotion, atrophy of imagination, subversion of order, and ruination of the mind." (Ibid., p. 198) The author writes that in the "hidden symbolism" of the two short-stories (Filidor and Filibert) one discovers "the final, secret meaning of this work" (Ibidem); there is a convention in this confession too and we are left only with the task of detecting this book's role of preparing other narrative and dramatic experiences, placed in the service of meditation and of provoking the reader called to discover the epic literature's new connections in time.

***

"Differently however, we somewhat broke loose from that fear which frightened us and which, like the veils of fog rising from the swamps, confuses the mind. That is why work hasn't left us when the Great Forester increased his powers in our region, and fear spread out everywhere." (Ernst Jünger, *Pe falezele de marmură*, Bucharest, Univers, 1971). The author of the wonderful *Paris Diaries* (1979), published only in 1997 in Romanian, wrote in 1939 a poem-book or, what could be called an allegory-book: *On the Marble Cliffs*. The destiny of the writers who remained in Germany after Adolf Hitler had become chancellor of the Reich and later the absolute "ruler" was far from easy. Neither Jünger escaped accusations after the end of the war, neither philosophers like Heidegger, who today is still analyzed with reserve given his adhesion, even if a partial and hesitant adhesion; however, *On the Marble Cliffs* is an evident allusive protest, in the sub-text, and "the Great Forester", the terrifying and disquieting ruler, is none other than Kniébolo from the *Diaries*, the dictator, a subject of discussions between the great writer and his closest friends.

Furthermore, Jünger's *Diaries* are symptomatic for the status of the writers forced to an inner exile, experiencing a permanent soliloquy, evoking the memory of fundamental books and rediscovering, under the sign of the tragic, the sentiment of friendship and solidarity, as well as that of their writing's *ethos*. Including intimate, secrete notes from 1941 to 1944, the "books" of the *Diaries* celebrate another epiphany of the sacred book, the *Bible*, or of several works with archetypal value, such as *One Thousand and One Arabian Nights*. The echoes of several bloody events (the uprising of the Jews in Warsaw in 1943: "For the first time, they fought here like in the old days against Titus, or like the persecutions during the crusades", in Ernst Jünger, *Jurnale pariziene*, Bucharest, Humanitas, 1997); the unimaginable suffering of the Jews of the ghetto in Lodz; the evil's exorcism; the obsession of Dostoevsky's characters and, especially, of Stavroghin etc. are all painfully registered. The writer's "crises" are indeed alleviated by his Parisian status, by the meetings with French writers in the city's salons, by the walks taken on the streets of the decimated former capital of France, with second-hand bookshops explored by a warned reader.

Certainly, Ernst Jünger was right when he noted, often inspired by the maxims and aphorisms of Lichtenberg, that "Books, too need a good period of time to get rid of temporality. They too have their purgatory. Then they transcend the critique." (Ibid.). I do not know how much truth is in this affirmation; it is however certain that *On the Marble Cliffs* is a symbol-book for what the world was for the surrealists: "The world as a mental hospital built rationally" (*Paris Diaries*); the phrase made reference to the surrealists and to their forerunners: Lautréamont, Emily Brontë, Heinrich von Kleist. An attentive reflection on the book reveals motifs repeated in the *Diaries*: the solidarity of "those who work on books of the spirit" (*On the Marble Cliffs*); the auctorial narrator confesses that "*We used to live in times in which the author was condemned to loneliness*", and the artist was embraced by "the fear for the fate of our pages" (Ibid.). I do not think that the common leitmotif of the *pest* is a simple coincidence – a contagious malady overstepping any obstacles, admitting no immunized, secured space. The scourge extends and announces dangers for the consciences gravely threatened through and due to their lucidity. From *A Journal of the Plague Year* (1722) by Defoe to the allegory-novel *The Plague* (1947) by Albert Camus, the adventure becomes a cataclysm with symbolic, premonitory value; the enclosed universe, the crime, the isolation and the loneliness of the human being from Camus's novel are connected, to a certain extent, to the book *Narziss and Goldmund* (1930) by Hermann Hesse, which is based on the symbols of creation and of renouncement through reclusion and meditation. The journey, in Hesse's novel, and the itinerary of the fugitive from *The Horseman on the Roof* (1951), the extraordinary book by Jean Gino, the encounter with the tragic manifestation of death and desperation have a somewhat surprising correspondent in *The Skin* (1949), the novel by Curzio Malaparte, related to the terror and horror scenes from *Kaputt* - the reportage of intense drama signed by the same author.

In the work of the Italian writer, the pest extends to Naples, after the allied troops (American, French, Polish etc.) make their entry in the city. We witness a sight which seems to have sprung out of the plasticity of Bruegel and Bosch, out of the traumatizing and unforgettable images of the "Court of Miracles".

The remembrance of the picaresque novel

The model created by Robert Musil and Hermann Broch, the dramaturgy and prose of Hofmannsthal, as well as the entire German tradition (philosophy, religion, visual arts) of a literature undoubtedly influenced by the reform (Luther) and by the great creations of Goethe return to the attention of the writers in whose biography the years prior to World War II and, especially, the tragedy of the German people in the early months of 1945 become the object of reflection and especially of epic creation. I find the observation of the literary historian Fritz Martini about a certain retrieval of the contacts with foreign literatures rather questionable because the German narrativity has never lost its connections with other literatures, even if we consider the writers exiled in France, the country where numerous creators of German language (Robert Musil, Hermann Hesse) found refuge or lived till the end of their lives. Then again, there is a really important true fact: the discovery of the work of Franz Kafka; however, the phenomenon is valid for the European literature in general, especially following the end of World War II. As we know it very well by now, Kafka's influence would be decisive although the writers did not strictly follow the formula of the absolutely poly-semantic novel, the ambiguity of the narrative space and time, of the symbols and of a vast semiotization of narrative invariants (the character, the a-historism, the temporal indetermination etc.).

Unquestionably, the influence and overwhelming personality of Thomas Mann will also impress the post-war generations of novelists. The novel *Doctor Faustus*, with the subtitle "The Life of the German Composer Adrian Leverkühn, As Told by a

Friend" (1947), might have not been necessarily taken as a model by the new German writers, but rather as a warning for responsibility, artistic conscience and cultural destiny in a country so hardened, and subjugated by a terrorizing dictatorship. The invitation to reflection – we could also include here Hermann Hesse – and to analysis, to a brutal and honest examination represents, I believe, an essential term for the post-war German literature. At its core, the placement of "Group 47" seems totally legitimate to me.

The reading of the works of Günter Grass or the creations of Heinrich Böll (both are reputable authors of short-stories, novels and essays); likewise, the prose of Martin Walser and of Alfred Andersch or the creation of Heimito von Doderer (short-stories, accounts and novels) generate a strong impression on the readers due to the dramatic quality of the works, the tension of the motifs and of the imagined destinies, due to the dimension of the epic fiction open to express often unforgiving truths, due to the history and the evolution of a betrayed humanity, captured by lies and by a radical ideology, with decidedly grave consequences for the destiny of the German people. A feeling of guilt; the acute condemnation of the past and the conscience of a necessary culpability are found in representative works, extremely diverse given their approaches, their artistic formulas and narrative sources. The tragic, the grotesque and the enormous comic; the satirical attack and the buffoonery; irreconcilable and untreatable conflicts – motifs of a world barely surviving the nightmare of the war; the compromises and the hypocrisy, the temptation to forget and to justify the crimes are as many aspects which have entered the areas of imaginary and fiction, both inexhaustible as regards the chosen approaches. The appeal to lucidity and to sanctioning the still-evident tares and the right to a new existence are frequently included in the post-war literature. A historical fact is also rather significant: some writers belong to a more distant era; they witnessed the events before and during World War I; they then had to live the experimenting years that followed this human cataclysm; they observed the social tormenting, the ascension of National-Socialism, the brutal German occupation of Austria in

1938 (*Anschluss*) and then the disaster of the war.

Such a perspective, relived in literary creations modeled and inspired by various programs (the expressionism had undoubtedly a decisive influence!), could not but have fertile consequences. Furthermore, the tradition will affect those who entered the Austrian and German literary life with their memories of children and teenagers raised under the dominion of the Nazi propaganda and dementia. Traumatized, survivors of the shipwreck of a Germany condemned by the world's nations, they continue or start a literary career of revisions, crises and moral shudders. Such factors had probably stimulated literary searches and experiments, and the novel and the dramaturgy were the beneficiaries of the intellectual biographies matured through suffering and through the revelation of a new human solidarity. There are also other writers, like Heimito von Doderer, with a memory filled with the events of two world wars; they had thus traveled through the inferno's bowges and revealed to their contemporaries the apocalyptic paths of the journey towards the disaster of downfalls or towards the lights of salvation...

In his "Preface" (a true study) to *Ein Umweg* (Heimito von Doderer, *Drum cotit*, Bucharest, E.L.U., 1967), Dieter Schlesak refers to Doderer's misfortune of not having received an immediate appraisal, just like it happened to Franz Kafka or to his contemporaries Robert Musil and Hermann Broch. Only after 1945 did their works gain the attention of the readers thanks to the French and American translations. Thus, today they are known authors mentioned not only in literary histories, but especially in the studies dedicated to the modern novel, a form ever more open to new narrative solutions and perspectives. As the German writer of Romanian origin emphasizes in his introductory study, Austria was for the generations of the abovementioned writers "a universe of spiritual life, whereas the strong contradictions of Austrian-like historical existence were the soil and paradoxically the «abyss» generating values that belong to universal literature and without which European culture would have been much poorer" (Schlesak, "Preface", in Doderer, 1967).

An aspect impossible to ignore is that Doderer – an active soldier in the two world wars - recreates an itinerary easily identifiable in the works of authors like Ernst Jünger for example. The author of novels and short-stories is, at the same time, a reputable and well-known theoretician of the novel, pleading for the "total novel" (Ibid.); in other words, he declares himself open and receptive to the solutions given by a great diversity of texts summed and assimilated within the protean and multiform novel, a free novel due to the rejection of unilateral formulas.

The symptoms presented in *The Man without Qualities* – the fall of the Empire and the degradation of authentic values, substituted by appearances and by the anachronic luxury of a world experiencing its downfall, a hypocrite and profoundly ignorant world - can be found in *The Demons*, the vast chronicle by Doderer. This is a novel where the *demonization* and the decomposition of the Austrian culture and society generally define a mediocre and philistine universe consonant with the reaction of a Mephistopheles drawn by these maladies.

It is the "demonism of mediocrity", of an irrepressible, fatal current without salvation: "Everything which is self-evident is a monster that sleeps next to us. Now the beast is awakening, it's moving. I have recognized it." (Ibid.).

This is the constant and essential message of Musil's or of Broch's creations.

Far older, Heimito von Doderer experienced the war, as I have already pointed out, as a fighter (during the 1940s), whereas a novelist barely formed after the war, Heinrich Böll, experienced tough battles and was wounded several times; for five years his biography had fused with the fights on the battlefronts of one of the most absurd wars in the world. I consider his first novel, *Where were you, Adam?*, a unique book given its history dominated by the absurd characteristics of the adventure lived by a German soldier at the time of the retreating armies' desegregation, a soldier who left the continuously moving battlefront, conscious of the inevitable end of Germany, and who finally arrived close to his native village and house. The questions, the drifting, the acute feeling of the ending and of the uselessness of the endured sufferings reach their climax at the moment of his return when, a German battery, the only one still left on the collapsing western front, kills him – absurd sacrifice of this drifting world. Böll confirms an excellent (by now) science of the trauma and of dosing the situations according to the dramatism of the narrative scenario.

Polemic and rather cynical, Heinrich Böll examines the "new" Germany of ruins and rebirth; *House without Guardians* (1954), *Billiards at Half-past Nine* (1959) and especially *The Clown* (1963), cruel to the clergy, to the new political class, to the hypocrisy and the amnesia of the people willing to forget easily the crimes' authors and their own guilty participation. Heinrich Böll's works tell the "story" of dysfunctional families, of individuals sickened by the fears and nightmares of a society still chased by the ghosts of the past, thus making him a remarkable personality. He conjugates the prose of detailed and refined drama with pages which seem to be related, through referents animated by the novelist, to the literary reportage or to the diary – a diary recording all anxieties and cataclysms. In general, the writers grouped in that "front" of literary militarism ("Group 47") have an exaggerated acuity and sensibility when they refer to the war's victims and consequences: condemned destinies, orphans, crippled and witnesses, bombed towns turned into ruins by the American and British air forces, the dubious ascension of certain people who got rich thanks to the war etc. "I have always wanted to write", confesses Heinrich Böll, "I had first tried it when I was very young but I only found the words later" (in Mariana Şora, "Preface" to Heinrich Böll, *Casa văduvelor*, Bucharest, E.P.L., 1965). This "discovery" of words has the value of a necessary justification of perspective, the establishment of a *Weltanschauung* based on an insight into and a lucid evaluation of the events, of the stigmatized period between the 1930s to the 1950s.

It would be difficult to accept the phenomenon "Group 47" without reminding the readers that, in addition to the propaganda literature, in addition to the films aimed at deluding and influencing those behind the battlefronts, in addition to the propagandistic arsenal used in World War II, there also were works of deep tragedy, among which the novel *The Tin Drum* (1959) by

Günter Grass. I find it to be one of the most profound creations dedicated to the *tragic-grotesque memory* of a bizarre witness: a dwarf playing the role of commentator, possessing among his memories and on the rhythm of the drum/drums the diagram of an entire period of tumultuous history, with changes and situation overthrows placed on a complicated itinerary filled with signs which are sometimes hilarious, other times comical or grotesque manifestations, but which are always tragic in the end. The impression it gives is of watching one of Brecht's plays with the pieces inspired by the manifestations of the Third Reich: *Mother Courage and Her Children, Fear and Misery of the Third Reich, The Resistible Rise of Arturo Ui* etc. A product of a crazy era, having spent his childhood years in Danzig (Gdansk), still not seized by the German troops, watching and testifying through the rhythms of the ever-present drum, maturing and sickly listening to the events' description, to their recount, substantiated by his own adventures, Oskar Matzerath is the symbol of a mutilated age (suffering from dwarfism and deformed like a clown from the late Middle Ages), interpreting the role of a sad character, who experienced serious affairs. This is the time of a literature defined by the use of the grotesque and the caricature, of the discovery of those hideous phenomena generating suffering worlds.

The developments during the 1940s-1950s; the capitulation of Nazi Germany; the disembarking of the allied troops in Europe; the war in the Pacific constituted the map of famous narratives like *The Skin* (1949) by Curzio Malaparte, the novel of the liberated Naples - the city of a plague even more terrifying than the malady itself (the novel has obvious connections with his far more notorious work, *Kaputt*, published in 1945, a reportage with multiple transgressions of reality into a fictional universe, absolutely memorable and of great stylistic beauty, a creation from the famous series of "frenetic" reportages launched by Egon Erwin Kisch and continued by writers such as Norman Mailer or the Romanian Geo Bogza). Norman Mailer is the author of the novel *The Naked and the Dead* (1948), a narrative of brutal, violent realism about the war in the Pacific seen from the perspective of a group of soldiers observed throughout the tension of the fights, lacking any heroism, any patriotic-like mumblings of some other pages written in the post-war period.

Actually, the representation of this international catastrophe is registered remarkably in a few works significant for the post-Stalin Russian literature. An extraordinary generation of novelists follows the great tradition of Lev Tolstoy, Dostoevsky or Chekhov, firmly rejecting the toned-down image of a finally real, suffering Russia. Andrei Bitov, Fyodor Abramov, Viktor Astafiev, Vasili Belov and especially Valentin Rasputin excite today's readers due to the depth and authenticity used in the creation of the atmosphere, of the individual's drama in a world alienated from the human moral values. *Live and Remember* by Rasputin could have a correspondent in the novel by Heinrich Böll *Where were you, Adam?*. The book's plot evolves around the destiny of Andrei Guskov, a wounded Siberian soldier who decided not to return on the battlefront, around his fears and his terrifying loneliness, around his consuming love for Nastiona, who was forced to share by sacrifice the fate of her husband. This is what Heinrich Böll will name, via the comments of his narrator ingratiated in the script of the novella *The Train was on Time*, "the terrifying and at the same time staggering force of destiny" (in Heinrich Böll, *Destinul unei ceşti de cafea*, Bucharest, Univers, 1968).

I have to say that not only the novelist Heinrich Böll has the right to be invoked; any reference to his work also focuses on his short-stories; one of the most successful as regards the development of the "journey" towards death, the tension and perception of the main character's obsessions, is the abovementioned short-story. *The Train was on Time* is the itinerary towards death of a young German soldier who went on the eastern front, an itinerary obstructed by the obsession with death ("I don't want to die, this is horrifying, because I don't want to die", Böll, 1968). The word, observes the narrator situated close to the soldier's anxieties and premonitions, "suddenly gets a secret meaning", registering the fear's shudders, the tremors of the night journey - "and fear was buried deep, deep inside of him" (Ibid.). The nocturnal landscape (eliminating the diurnal; the self-rediscovery), "the cadaverous fingers of the spotlights", the leitmotif of the *wall*, the symbol of an overwhelming obstacle beyond which lies death, the somber premonition of death, the delimitation realized through naming some nocturnal figures ("a railway station without a sound voice", Ibid.), the permanent alternation and (sometimes) juxtaposition of layers create the atmosphere of a memorable text. The images follow or overlap one another in the agitated and profoundly disturbed memory of the main character: the Jews of Chernowitz and the Jews of Lemberg; isolated words included in this demented mosaic, shaken by the shadows of death, turn Andreas's journey, the soldier touched by the death signs, into the unique and symbolic adventure of the approaching ending. The apocalypse exists within the individual sent to death just like on a journey toward an inexorable inferno.

I have already stated that this is a novella and – it is a known fact – the novella has in its Benedictine austerity, in the perfect tuning of its components a careful surveillance within the genre of the composition, of the rhythms and analytical design of the characters invited/forced to analyze themselves up to the last signs of the subconscious. Hence, the concentrated placement into abyss of the characters' inner movement, the crowdedness of the elements meant to generate the *atmosphere*, the multiple connotations of the discourse, the nature of the sentences and the observation of some elements aimed at fixing the spiritual environment of the heroes.

The Train was on Time is an exemplary text depicting the universe of a drifting world, projecting a time of death, suffering and disaster. The war and the recollection of certain events; the frustration and the paroxysmal; the absurd and the absurd environment of death haunt the German writers. An interesting detail is the irrepressible feeling of guilt, of crime. A Romanian-born writer, Dieter Schlesak, reminisces in an episode meant to draw again the attention on the supreme sensibility of the conscience troubled by the most absurd (and at the same time tragic) confessions of the years preceding the end of a Germany led – not without the consent and frenzy of the German people – to downfall and condemnation. In the volume "*Days at Home* and the Art of Disappearance" ("*Zile acasă* and *Arta dispariției*", published by the Romanian Cultural Foundation in 1995), the novelist re-lives the impressions and feelings of a German man who returned in his Transylvanian *burg*, constantly inserting moments of his experiences in Germany. An episode organized epically with a remarkable dosage of the plot narrates an event that took place in a "wretched" village in Germany where on 10 April 1945 three peasants (the mayor and another two citizens), in order to avoid the destruction of their village (the American tanks were right outside the village), are accused of betrayal, condemned to death and hanged by a unit of *Hitlerjungen* (Hitler Youth) and SS troops... The terrified people witness the execution and the existing commemorative inscription testifies for a moment of tragic history, observing the desperation and deformation of a nation governed by the dementia of the hangmen. Just like other German novelists, Dieter Schlesak probably asked himself the question that unfortunately had become a cliché: how was it possible? How could these hangmen thrive, transformed in mere automats ready to execute the abominable deeds, without any hesitation, without any trace of emotion?

The questions did not remain just rhetorical phrases; the etiology of the crime and of its followers, as well as the phenomenology of terror and of its constant refinement do not belong only to the Nazi regime that had gained power in Germany in 1933. Far earlier, the German-language literature (Austrian, German, Swiss etc.) drew the attention on and projected the ever more obvious and the ever more serious signs of a world apparently willing to start the play of the downfall, announcing its own apocalypse. *From Thomas Mann or Heinrich Mann to Robert Musil and Hermann Broch, the literature rediscovered the raison d'être of meditation and of a high and deep intellectualization of writing.* Without them, the truths could not have been uttered with such a dramatic force. In a world touched by the agents of evil, *within the space and time of a demonism* seized by irrepressible frenzy, the literature warned, analyzed and *decreed the regime of the reflection's lucidity* so that the narrative invariants, the event, the narrative stances, the characters, the plot, the climax of the epic action, the composition's logic and the interpretation's instruments (the play, the parody, the satire, the irony, the derision, an inexhaustible set of linguistic and non-verbal signs) could draw the attention on the downfall into nothingness.

Related to the acknowledged forms of literary reportage, the book by Günter Grass *Crabwalk* (*Im Krebsgang*) was published in 2002 (Göttingen, Steidl Berlag). It is a significant work, a study devoted to the poetics of reflexive prose, animated by the density and experience of the captivating, passionate epic account open to confrontations with the reader; firstly, because it re-estates the supremacy of memory, of decanting and of the epic re-experiencing of a utterly tragic event. The narration obviously is related to the resources and forms of literary reportage: a blend of authentic events, verifiable, confirmed by the circumstances recorded at the moment of the incidents' development, and by fictional availabilities, absolutely indispensable for re-experiencing, within an imaginary space, the human behaviors and mechanisms, all the events set under the key of recollection.

In 1945 (the precise date is recorded: January, 30th), a German passenger ship, "Wilhelm Gustloff", left the Danzig harbor with a few thousand refugees on board: the majority of whom were mothers and children to be transported to Western Germany; the ship was sunk by a Soviet submarine and thus, more than four thousand people died in the Baltic waters... The history of this tragic event is put together through multiple references and numerous digressions, having a reconstituting purpose (the reportage professes frequently the *reconstitution* based on data connected via the narrative fiction), accompanied by the voice and comments of the *raisonneur-reporter*.

The questions multiply, creating the stimulating pretext for reminiscences and, more precisely, for the *epic reconstruction* of that moment difficult to forget. The "exteriorized" monologue of the narrator does not justify or, to be more accurate, does not absolve from a given amnesia or delay; the desperate cry, the scream and the lamentation reclaim their words, the *digging up* of the past and the return through flash-backs to biographies, situations, events unspared from coincidences or surprising connections. The narrator remains faithful to the formula ratified over time by the German prose: *irony* and *sarcasm*, the sad encounter with the times' monstrosities, with hideous biographies for the outraged and aggressed memory of the witness-narrator, descendent of those who existed.

The temporal distance (more than half a century from that death-end in the Baltic waters) and the duty to pass through time like a crab's step are the terms (*chronotope*) of this history. Günter Grass does not betray his predecessors: the book merges the forms of the reportage with those of the epic narrative and *the comments claim now the technology of the internet*. The deposited memory, the extended and multiplied information, the association of certain facts, situations and events with resonances in the historic time etc. are set through the appeal to computerized technology ("I found these details, as well as others, on the internet", states the narrator).

Actually, the history of the shipwreck (the German refugees who arrived in Danzig and then were boarded on the "Wilhelm Gustloff" to arrive in a western harbor on the coastline of the Baltic Sea) assimilates accents and autobiographical references inserted intentionally in the text from the perspective of the poetics of the *narrative reportage* (the constantly evoked experience of his mother who had been among the passengers rescued after the ship's bombing by the Soviet submarine *S 13* commanded by the marine officer Alexander Marinesko). Thus, the impression of lived history, restored through accumulating confessions, data, archives, press accounts about a trial in a Swiss court is increased. The sum of situations is dosed and filtered scholarly; the information distributed according to the logic of the internet ("I pulled out information that was accessible to me..."), whereas the reporter – the writer with journalist experience – constructs in the space of the imaginary, simulating or simply redoing mentally the succession of circumstances with surprisingly numerous time references belonging to the memory of the last war years, 1943-1944.

The journalist does not reject various hypotheses or variants. He builds according to the laws of narrative fiction a system of referents extremely well designed and compiled. The memory of

World War II, charged with crimes, absurd situations and cruelty, is reanimated in this apparently singular book; in reality, it is consonant with the spirit of the German literature presided by Musil, Broch or Thomas Mann, continued and developed by the generation of Günter Grass, by the writers of that group that had entered the history of German literature under the well-known name of "Group 47". The data are communicated, according to the effects of the scenario and of the plot, through calculated oppositions, through the use of the oxymoron as stylistic figure appropriately justified: more than 4,000 new-born babies or toddlers; around 100 rescued; commander Marinesko ends his biography with years of detention in a labor camp in Kolyma!...; the launching of the "Wilhelm Gustloff" in the presence of the Führer etc. The leitmotif is that of the *imagination* called upon to build in an apparently disorganized, arbitrary structure. The *entropy* is reclaimed by the contextual suggestion of the chaos, the confusion, the fear of the desperate shipwrecked people.

Heterogeneous and often heteroclite, the information, the situations, the potential characters (the witnesses and the heroes of the scenario/scenarios), the chronicle of the events, the press coverage, the archives converted in the memory of the computer, they all account for the events putting them together according to a mechanism related rather to cinema (documentaries). Günter Grass is, in the end, the witness-narrator, the chronicler, the reporter drawn rather by the ironic, caustic and constantly skeptical commentary. Unwilling to forget, forced to relive for the memory of the Family and to advance an invitation to meditation about the aberrations, the absurd, the tragic and grotesque ironies of History, itself the somber and sad stage of the World. The data are precise (the internet...), 5 May 1937: the launching of the ship in the presence of Adolf Hitler who had arrived to the event with a special train and who then saluted the enthusiastic crowd from a convertible Mercedes; the happy workers who were there and who had, years before, voted with the socialists and the communists... Now they had the Führer, they had Robert Ley, the artisan of the cruise ship; on 24 March 1938 one thousand Austrians enjoyed a trip with the ship later known as the "Wilhelm Gustloff", only fifteen days before the *Anschluss* – the act of Austria's disappearance!...; finally, history ends, the history inaugurated by Musil, about the end of an empire and of a World, of Kakania... Then there is the chronicle of the war: the beginning of the disaster (Stalingrad), the ruins of the German towns after the American-British bombardments and, finally, after years of suffering, the fall of the Berlin wall!

Many other scenes are recollected in an amazing composition of extraordinary evoking force (the accumulation and insertion of events found later on the websites): the survivors' meeting after the fall of the Berlin wall; the remembrance of the ordeal of the refugees in Oriental Prussia, the procession of the desperations and the death coming from snow storms ("the white death").

The disorder and the abandonment of the events' chronology (flash-backs) are part of the cinematography, of the sequences edited according to the dramatic characteristics and to the logic of the demonstration. In such situations, the organization of a true suggestive background with multiple references becomes necessary, placing the characters and justifying their hidden or less understandable connections. The movement is typical of theatre or film, having a number of *dramatis personae*, not necessarily announced according to the theatrical tradition but prepared to position the pinnacle moments of the narrative reportage. Wilhelm Gustloff, a Nazi with missions in Switzerland, with a biography aimed at explaining the name of the ship launched in 1937, and David Frankfurter, the young Jew who took refuge in Switzerland after the humilities experienced in Germany and who is also Gustloff's assassin, are placed in the centre of the plot and their short biographies explain like in an anamnesis the history of the tragic shipwreck, reminisced by the novelist-reporter, a sardonic and caustic commentator, a cynical evoker of the events and of the names, of the history pages of the Third Reich ruled by the Führer acclaimed by a nation more or less convinced of its guiltiness but willing to forget the crimes either through suspicious amnesias, or through the cynicism of the future entrance on the political stage of Federal or Eastern Germany.

However, to assume again the "use of the internet", the documents deposited in the memory of the device do not generate literature, and the reporter becomes a writer only through narrative fiction; namely, the recreation of the facts through multiple combinations and through the confusing collage of names and events. Wilhelm Gustloff is sent to Davos (see Hans Castorp) to take care of his health; the affirmation of national-socialism makes him join the party and become an important factor among the Germans living in Switzerland. Like his forerunners or contemporaries, Günter Grass relives History like a capricious chronicle; the names and the events intervene and testify according to the sarcastic comments of the narrator: the irony is diffused following the biography of this Nazi alongside the names of Gregor Strasser or Robert Ley, leaders of Nazi workers' organizations, with the inoculated fanaticism, with the Night of the Long Knives. Therefore, Gustloff is the hideous standpoint, a deplorable Nazi figure (Hans Castorp from *The Magic Mountain* will be forced to leave Davos to loose himself among the rambles of World War I).

Moreover, the novelist confesses the History's acute and direct perception, guided by his flair and sensibility, to recognize the *signs of History*. It is the same manner of regarding the virtue of a demystifying and revealing vision; the events regain their hidden meaning; the Nazi rhetoric is disclosed and the doctrine's representatives are seen in the context of a denouncing and evident play. I have stated before that the autobiographical references are necessary for their involvement to acquire a distinctive effect, totally assuming the roles of accuser and commentator. Remembering and judging seem a condition of the compulsory lucidity needed by a real bench of magistrates, just like the way in which the narrator will apply it through the play imagined in *The Tin Drum*, where Oskar Matzerath, the buffoon-dwarf, will become the interpreter of the events announced via the drumbeats of a child and teenager suffering from dwarfism. Here, the reporter-commentator remakes a tragic event in order to retrieve other confessions and other resorts of history, with new and unusual depositions.

David Frankfurter, forced to take refuge in Switzerland given the Jews' situation in Germany – the internet further celebrates the role of gathering information -, assassinates the Nazi activist Wilhelm Gustloff, the "martyr" after whom will be named the cruise ship struck in 1945 by the torpedoes of the submarine commanded by Alexander Marinesko. Professing "creative writing", gathering information (the biography of the young Frankfurter), alternating the historic time and composing in a rhythm typical of a sensational reportage, Günter Grass will often clarify the facts, denouncing the bitter irony of the name carried by a ship destined to disappearance and death; the overbidding of the context (the "martyr" Gustloff); the insertion into the scenario of Marinesko (so that the plot can be taken to the end), the submarine's commander, born in Odessa of a Romanian father from around the region (a place with resonance for Eisenstein's film, "Battleship Potemkin"), are part of the composite structure, extremely open to references and digressions. Only now does the plot order its interpreters and assigns to them a special place in this equation relevant for the numerous confessions collected thanks to the internet. And the auctorial narrator comments that it all happened because the Jew Frankfurter managed to aim accurately and kill Gustloff, because at that time a ship was being built in Hamburg, which would carry his name and because a navy officer, Marinesko, was on duty on a submarine and because on 9 December 1936 began, in a cantonal courthouse in Switzerland, the trial of the assassination of Wilhelm Gustloff; the narrator will remake the history of a tragic ending: the death of approximately four thousand children in the Baltic waters...

The history, history again, will come back accompanied by the sounds and the rhythms of the "tin drum", and the destiny of Oskar Matzerath will allow the reader to observe the solidarity of a writers' generation through literary works always inspired by the tradition's critical, polemic and vigorous spirit, but also by the spirit of the XX century, so agitated and so close to the signs of the Apocalypse.

***

Remembrance and self-referentiality are present as "diggers" of memory and of answers to the question put by the narrative self: Oskar Matzerath. The history of this gnome attached to a hospital bed and surveyed by Bruno, his warden and guardian, evokes the models of the German picaresque novel, the curious "histories" related by the unique taste of the story-teller listened with amazement and admiration: "I, Bruno Münsterberg, of Altena in Saurland, [...], am a male nurse in the private pavilion of the local mental hospital. Mr. Matzerath, [...] is my patient. [...] Today, in order to rest his overstrained fingers, he has asked me to write for him [...]."; thus, according to the abovementioned medieval model, "Mr. Matzerath's story, [...] «Refugee from the East»" is born (Günter Grass, *The Tin Drum*, Vintage Random House, 2005; p. 400). Published in 1959, *The Tin Drum* belongs to the same aesthetic program reiterated by his contemporaries of "Group 47". It is the same taste for the enormousness originating in the tradition of Grimmelshausen, of a new... thirty-year war recounted with humor and with a tendency for using the grotesque mask. Furthermore, the gnome reedits the memorable figures of the buffoons from the royal courts.

The alternated play of the story and of the story-tellers, the intervention of the reflection about the events or generated by the nature of the narrative discourse, the open and (sometimes) labyrinth-like space of the imaginary, the hyperbole or the litote, the augmentation and the rediscovery or observation of the minute details make *The Tin Drum* an emblematic book; it can be placed *beyond* the never traditional, classic, "Balzac-like" realism of the German literature illuminated and ruled by the playful spirit of the ironic or hermetic philosopher, tempted by mask and parody, by allegory or parabola, by the metaphor of writing and thinking: Georg Christoph Lichtenberg.

Between the main character's monologue (the ostentatiously displayed self-referentiality), the presence of the auctorial narrator and the intervention of other characters (narrative voices directly announced), the discourse is modulated, it experiences metamorphoses or it proclaims the play and the parody: "Without bothering to read over what Bruno my keeper has written, I,

Oskar, take up my pen again." (Grass, 2005, p. 409); other times, the same narrator explains himself by creating narrative intervals surprising for the reader and for the narrative's rhythm (the tempo): "But for me, Oskar Matzerath Bronski Yorick, a new era was dawning, and scarcely aware of it, I took another quick look at Hamlet's worn-out fingers on the blade of my shovel" (Ibid., p. 437). The biography of the philosopher- and buffoon-gnome, a juggler equipped for surprising movements, events and incidents, is told in the variant of an "*Ich*-novel" doubled by the heterodiegetic narrative, free in connections and correspondences: "And so Yorick did not become a good citizen, but a Hamlet, *a fool*" (My emphasis added, ibid., p. 438). A narrative where the analepsis and the prolepsis – to use the terms and interpretations of Gérard Gennette (see Jaap Lintvelt, *Punctul de vedere. Încercare de tipologie narativă*, Bucharest, Univers, 1994) – are frequently designed to determine the narrative's perspective and tempos (the discourse's rhythms and not its chronology), is based on mix elements: narrative elements and, through simulation, reportage elements; the day, the hour, the moments of the action's development etc. use the *analepsis* to maintain above all a tight, intimate relation with the previous elements.

Such components are understandable in a novel where the narrator is involved, reliving and redistributing the events, gaining in his memory references for other "circles" of the recollections: when he was 21 years old, Oskar Matzerath, isolated in an asylum, reconstructs every episode of this epos experienced under the sign of the grotesque and of the masks' grimace. The scenes lived with the actors Roswitha Raguna and Bebra (a variant of the *world's theatre*), themselves suffering of dwarfism, their hilarious tour on the coast of the Atlantic through the fortifications of the "Atlantic wall", which would prove vulnerable, belong to a picaresque journey rediscovered like in a parodied "Divine Comedy", turning the book's protagonist into a sort of a witness to the breakdown of the false edifice of a Germany heated by its ruler's dementia. *The Tin Drum* gives the main character an identity typical of the *Bildungsroman*: a leitmotif of the book is Matzerath's formation. Having a passion for two books, he takes them everywhere with him: Goethe's *The Elective Affinities* and a book about hawking where Rasputin's tenebrous "stories" are told: "I didn't want to stake everything on Rasputin, for only too soon it became clear to me that in this world of ours every Rasputin has his Goethe, [...]." (Ibid., p. 78).

The history of the war's start and developments is thus written by a *buffoon* and his perspective deforms, increases or diminishes, focusing on scenes, people, situations, on the events' chronicle; in a word, the *view* forbids its own neutrality, the "objectivity". On the contrary, a world lost in itself, a world betrayed or easily deceived unfolds under the eyes of the reader through the indirect commentary of an interpreter always ready to simulate the "madness" of the buffoon or to fix on his face the clown's mask. Günter Grass is a non-negotiable novelist, not willing to accept the conventions of classic realism; his spectacle is raw, of unique ferocity, demystifying or repressing any wave of sentimentalism, even when it is a matter of the imaginary created around his own biography: his grandmother, the Koljaiczek family, Jan Bronski, Maria, the alleged son of Matzerath etc.

The picaresque novel relives its memorable moments in a new genre, telling extraordinary things to the fascinated, captivated or amused listener/reader; the style is intensified, it proliferates through word accumulations and series of characterizations, while the commentary – difficult to interrupt – is violent and hard, of supreme sharpness. Even the child's memory, with unpredictable associations and unexpected correspondences, registers in the same kind of disorganized discourse, like in an increasingly threatening avalanche: "Little people and big people, Little Claus and Great Claus, Tiny Tim and Carolus Magnus, David and Goliath, Jack the Giant Killer and, of course, the giant; I remained the three-year-old, the *gnome*, the Tom Thumb, the pigmy, the Lilliputian, the midget, whom no one could persuade to grow. [...] To avoid playing the cash register I clung to my drum and from my third birthday on refused to grow my so much a finger's breadth." (My emphasis added, ibid., p. 46).

If I were to take it a step further, I would say that it is not only a matter of a *referential time*, generous at any rate and filled with numerous events, people and places, but it also refers to a *historic time*, introduced through insertions commentated by the narrator; furthermore, we could add *another temporal level*, where the events have the role (but also the effect!) of scenes taken from a screenplay for a film based mostly on close-ups. The 1936 Berlin Olympic Games and the victories of Owens; events "of last year" (the analepsis intervenes frequently to restore the temporal levels and layers); a word attracts magnetically a far-from-innocent comment, the bitter irony denouncing and demystifying: the church *cross* is the passions' cross, the cross of St. Andrew, the Maltese cross, crosses with crutches or "de Gaulle's cross" - the cross of Lorena, and unfortunately the "yellow cross" worn by Jews - the prolepsis is illustrative, anticipating the dramas to come (Ibid., pp. 124-125. The narrative flux is often frenetic, irrepressible, introducing the commentary with multiple referential elements. It is what I call the "inter-referential" commentary. Because the German novelist does not ignore his predecessors, the way he does not ignore the caustic and the skeptical insight of the XVIII century German philosopher even when the related situations belong to his family universe (the grandmother, the mother, the hospital, and then the war: "[...] Poland was not yet lost [it was 1939], almost lost, and finally, at the end of those famous eighteen days, Poland was lost, although [...] Poland was not yet lost", ibid., p. 233).

The scenes multiply; it seems that they mix with other short "photograms", so that the memory does not lose any image: "O insane cavalry!" (Ibidem), and fragments from that desperate attack of the Polish cavalry: "There are the Uhlans, they've got the itch again, amid haystacks – another picture for you – wheeling their horses, they gather round a man, his name in Spain is Don Quixote" (Ibidem). Who sees in *The Tin Drum* a mere narrative history obsessed with the war and with its human implications commits a serious and unjustified error because the novel belongs, irreducibly, to the genre of narrative forms and of the History interpreted not by a winner but by a looser willing to attack and to prefer the mask of this gigantic human carnival of a pathetic melodrama with characters, war scenes and (shocking!)

bravery acts. The biography of Oskar Matzerath includes various facts inserted via the refusal of the cinematographic diary chronicle: "In the heat of August – I believe that the successful conclusion of another battle of encirclement, that from Smolensk" (Ibid., p. 282). And for the irony to be diffused through the connotative echo of the General Staff's message, the narrator records the baptism of Oskar's son, Kurt, like in a family diary.

History, as I said it before, is seen and interpreted parodically, the playfulness is more raw and poisonous than it would appear initially and in this heteroclite carnival, the buffoon does not forget to interleave some information placed in relations meant to change its dramatic or falsely dramatic character (for instance, the beginning of the invasion of June 1944). The comments seem to paraphrase, obviously parodically, years, events, locations, all charged with dramatic or tragic resonances and thus, Stalingrad (Matzerath utters the city's name, the starting point of the German failure, like he had done with places such as Pearl Harbor, Tobruk or "Dünkrichen" – it refers to Dunkerque, the harbor made famous in 1940 when the British troops and the rest of the French army were evacuated by ships on the open sea, following bloody clashes with the German troops). Not only allusively, the narrator continues, in the virtue of some illustrious models, commenting and animating the epic recount, assigning to it meanings detected by the reader as well. It is a parodied chronicle, like that of the wars evoked by Grimmelshausen and the voice of the chronicler-narrator, a primarily reflexive spirit, is harmonized with the moments lived under the sign of playfulness, of the dwarfs theatre (the "adventures" of Oskar Matzerath co-opted in the troop actors going on a tour of the German garrisons in the conquered France).

Each family event is analyzed by referring to the echo of the1943-44 battles. The scenes of the trip to the Atlantic coastline (1944) made with the other actors (Bebra, Roswitha Raguna, Felix, Kitty) are characterized by a Homeric enormity, like in the attempts of some gnomes called upon to announce the end of a stranded world. The epic formula professed by Günter Grass is visibly related to that of his companions of "Group 47", conjugating and interfering the individual destinies with those of a country experiencing a process of decomposition and fear: the pledged bombs sent over London; the definite breakdown of some families; the failed attempt to kill the Führer etc., they are all part of a history which is deliberately, I would say, hollowed, mutilated and deformed. It is, essentially, the way Günter Grass and his generation accustomed us: skeptical and disabused, cynical and undeniably pessimist in their lucidity, a true *defiance of History*. Not the disdain, but the sad grimace of the clown records and gives a certain configuration to the events: the flimsy front on the Vistula; Königsberg; the advancement of the Red Army and the terrorized people are not mere data often reminisced by the German writers of the same generation - witnesses (still young) or indirect victims of the Nazi dementia. The chronicle is designed through emphasizing the *ugliness* and the monstrousness. We observe again within the space of the German culture the *epiphany of negation*, of the brutal denouncing of evil and of that greedy animal that hides in a dark and demoniac past. The unimaginable suffering, the sacrifices, the nihilist spirit, the blasphemy are the symptoms of a rediscovering of the truth, of the intolerable.

A heterodiegetic narrator divides the narrative levels with the auctorial and the "actorial" narrators just like the homodiegesis is combined in a supple and highly mobile narrative: "[...] though today I am at home *neither in the sacred nor the profane* but dwell on the fringes, in a mental hospital." (My emphasis added, ibid., p. 131). The positioning between these levels and securing a special condition allow the narrator to develop various attitudes, inviting the characters to pass judgments (Bebra, Roswitha Raguna – the "somnambulist" from Naples), the gnomes having to bring in *The Tin Drum* the carnivalesque-tragic structure of the narrative guarded by a certain *infra-reality* (Oskar Matzerath had a gift to make sounds of such an incredible force that he broke stained-glasses, vases etc., thus having magic powers). Between divine and demonic, emphasizing the prose's relation to the German picaresque tradition, the narrative sometimes adopts the form of the diegesis, namely *the introduction into the story*: "There was once a musician, his name was Meyn, and he played the trumpet too beautifully for words" (Ibid., p. 190); or: "There was once a toy merchant, his name was Markus and he sold tin drums, lacquered red and white" (Ibidem), and going on with the story to suggest its infiniteness: "There was once a musician [...]"; There was once a watchmaker [...]" (Ibidem). Like a reader who returns to books close to his heart through numerous repetitions provoked and determined by the eternal, never abandoned or consumed acclamation of *story-telling*, I have the unutterable feeling of reading the English novelist Graham Swift, not only the writer of *Waterland* but also the author of other novels or essays dedicated to a supreme model such as Charles Dickens or examining the articulation and the magic of the timeless story-telling. Because even as regards Günter Grass and his *History is synonymous with Histrionics*, the world's sad spectacle is interpreted by the anonymous story-teller or the great blind man of the epos, by those who wrote *The Book of Kings* or about the miraculous and amazing destinies from *Estera* or *The Book of Judith*...

The skeptical and bitter narrator of Günter Grass is a chronicler involved not only "auctorially" and/or "actorially"; he is *the historian always unsatisfied with the times' signs* and, of course, neither with memory's signs as well: "I have just reread the last paragraph. I am not too well satisfied, but Oskar's pen ought to be [...]." (Ibid., p. 228). The surprise is that of the creation and of the narrative levels' structuring and the novelist is, each time, a narrator who provokes and instigates. Oskar Matzerath seems to accompany the hoards of hungry soldiers, embittered by the three decades of medieval war, evoked more than once by German writers. I feel like reading Brecht and the story of *Mother Courage and Her Children*, in the drama subtitled by the author "A Chronicle from the Thirty-Year War" and where Anne's song begins with the lyrics: "Let the drums quiet down / damn this war" (Bertolt Brecht, *Teatru*, E.S.P.L.A., 1958). The (today) forgotten play-writer surely has numerous reasons related to the voice, the vision and the atmosphere of the German literature liberated from any constraints and fears at the end of World War II.

In the character of the gnome, Günter Grass imagined a terrible allegory of a mutilated and disfigured world. "While slipping into his clothes, adjusting the drum around his neck, stowing his drumsticks under the braces, Oskar carried on negotiations with his two gods Dionysus and Apollo." (Grass, 2005, p. 304). And whereas the god of "unreflecting drunkenness" advises him to take with him (in any case) "a little stack of Rasputin" (the feuilleton novel frequently reread), the "shrewd" Apollo advises him not to forget (when he leaves for France with the troop of dwarf-actors) "the highly respectable yawn that Goethe had yawned so long ago" (Ibidem). He refers to *The Elective Affinities*, the other opposing title, among the character's preferences. Antonyms, "drunkenness" and "chaos" oppose "harmony", thus configuring the face prepared for the masks of the tragic and the grotesque, the masks always surveyed by the narrator's lucid and deeply reflexive commentary.

***

I wrote a book about a *different* novel or about a novel frequently encountered without allowing its forms to betray the defining structures of this narrative variant. And I am struggling because the experience of the writers I read or re-read attracts in an un-dissimulated manner other books, beyond the initial project, even though their dominant spirit seems to strictly digress in various ways from a given formula or poetics which I identified so far as: *essay-novel*, *meditation-novel*, *reflexive novel*, *novel of digressions and of incursions in the areas of lucidity and of concepts*; moreover, in order not to risk the emergence of potential confusions, it is appropriate to affirm the *supremacy of the novel as narrative structure based on the celebration of the story-telling and of the epic "histories"*, constantly reediting the archetype of the account and of the fable announced via that miraculous "Once upon a time...". Actually, the prolegomena (the poetics and the elements of narratology communicated by referring to the writers' various works and confessions) announced and warned about the *choice* made by the author of these pages. None of the analyses, none of the comments betrays the vocation and the supreme gift of story-telling. They generate the great eposes – great creations where the meditation and the people's destinies, people's actions and their anxious or troubled consciences all meet under the same protective god: the story-telling and the story-teller predestined by the gods to keep the memory of mankind in exchange for the suffering that the people have to bear.

The novel's poetics, to be more exact, the poetics of a certain type of novel is far from encouraging uniformity. By striving for the universal and the cosmic, the novel discovers its own great diversity, announced by Rabelais's masterpiece: *Gargantua and Pantagruel* realizes a world seen through the enormousness, through the Homeric and terrible laughter of the heroes, leaving for journeys and for battles, fighting with the University and with the clergy, with the philosophers from Sorbonne; it is a creation definitively confirmed by the sudden changes of the nights of the Sad Countenance from *Don Quixote*. From now onward, the picaresque novel, the novel of the sad adventures of Grimmelshausen's heroes, the novel born from the supreme "*ars combinatoria*" of Laurence Sterne, *Tristam Shandy*, consolidate the destiny of this literary form.

The novel's poetics is the least willing to accept exact definitions and precise rules. The novel challenges, provokes; it is the form which defies through diversity, through its changing, absorbing nature; *hence, the variants of the story-novel*, because to tell a story can also mean to meditate and to convince the characters to enter the superior game of the *idea*, of ghosts, of History and of the most unbelievable combinations – stances of an individual endowed with rationality, thinking and imagination.

Therefore, there are in this book reasons and novel alternatives able to bring together writers and their creations; betraying the German literature, we are more interested in the formula/formulas of the novel where the author and the narrator's alternatives celebrate *the reflexive insight*, the meditation as troubled and anxious echo of the events. This is the case of Curzio Malaparte and his novel *The Skin* (1949) or, beyond the discourse's pathos and the writer's so controversial and vulnerable ideological nature, Louis-Ferdinand Céline and his "German trilogy" (*Castle to*

Castle, 1957; *North*, 1960; *Rigodon*, published posthumously in 1969). The literary discourse's unmistakable differences of perspective, of assumed preference, of distinct proprieties do not reject their association under the protection of the same narrative phenomenon examined thus far.

Furthermore, except for the more or less funny episode of the conflict between Musil and Broch (the accusations advanced by the author of *The Man without Qualities*), it is difficult to imagine that the similarities of motifs and attitude, the professed *poetics* and the supremacy of the lucid, emblematic commentary could be flattened or equalized. The taxonomy, the criteria generated by the literary research operate only through approximations, entrusting the creation with its autotelic, original and therefore creative status. How do such creations relate to others, like *Ferdydurke* by Witold Gombrowicz to the superb allegorical history from *On the Marble Cliffs* by Ernst Jünger? In the equation of narrative structures, the *paradigm of the reflexive prose* is realized thanks to the narrator's mobility and according to the *choice* made by the novelist: auctorial or "actorial", proclaiming his self without any mediating elements; heterodiegetic or celebrating the told histories and summoning the narratar, often an implicit lecturer or simply an interpreter within the combinative mechanism of the epic game, the writer recognizes his own belonging to the prose ennobled by idea, by *the voice which thinks*.

This is the explanation for the "confirmation" and inclusion in this family of Malaparte's novel, *The Skin*: a "Curzio Malaparte" (the play and the conventions are also used in his famous reportage *Kaputt*), a liaison officer to the allied troops debarked in Italy and "infiltrated" in Naples, the captive-city seen in an age of *plague*, of terrible, unimaginable filth, keeping open all the wounds caused by Mussolini's regime. The entrance of the allied troops; the overwhelming sight of the guarded city, still threatened by the Vesuvius and by the feeling of the undeniable downfall of an apparently condemned nation, generates the bitter and cynical reflection of the narrator still tempted (and thus extending the reportages book from *Kaputt*) to demystify everything, to liberate Italy's image from the fog of earlier lies. The tragic and the grotesque, the horror and the carnivalesque – raw, violent, purulent – rule over the commentary about a city which has been in eternal slavery for twenty centuries... A Cartesian sarcasm erupts in the voice of the narrator determined to explain to the defeated the world of this unique Italian territory: "It is not enough to loose a war to have the right to consider oneself a defeated nation. Given their ancient wisdom, based on a painful centuries-long experience, my poor Neapolitans did not confer to themselves the right to feel defeated, undoubtedly, it was a serious want of tact" (Curzio Malaparte, *Pielea*, Bucharest, Univers, 2000); "Christ was from Naples" (Malaparte, 2000). Malaparte's interlocutor, the character of this book in which overlap (*an active, protean intertextuality*) fiction and a conventional reality of literary reportage, is Jack Hamilton, an unusually cultivated American officer, a different type of intellectual compared to the writers met in Paris in 1925: Ernest Hemingway, Sinclair Lewis, Ezra Pound and many others: "However, Jack wasn't one of those *Americains de Paris* ever-present in *The Sun also Rises* by Hemingway, who in 1925 used to hang around Select in Montparnasse, who used to despise having tea at Ford Maxon Ford and the bookshop Sylvia Beach and about whom Sinclair Lewis, regarding certain characters by Eleanor Green, said that they were «like some intellectual refugees from Rive Gauche around 1925 or like T. S. Eliot, Ezra Pound or Isadora Duncan, *iridescent flies caught in the black web of an ancient and amoral European culture*», Jack wasn't even one of those young decadent from the other side of the Atlantic, gathered around the American magazine *Transition* which was being published in Paris in 1925. No, Jack wasn't a «déraciné», or a decadent, he was an American who had fallen in love with Europe." (Ibid.).

The novel has often the tonality of a creation of a moralist determined to communicate more convincingly and more captivatingly via a narrative dominated by the fiction's open territories. The x-raying of the city, ever more degraded like in an allegory of the downfall into the World's nothingness, is extraordinary and Curzio Malaparte (the novelist and not the character!) realizes one of the most terrifying and moving representations of that decomposition: the poverty, the prostitution, the Virgin Mary exposed for the amazement of the American or Moroccan soldiers, tempted to verify, vaginally, the virginity... An Italian patriotism harbored in the pubis, observes bitterly and in a disabused manner the *raisonneur*-narrator, he too contaminated by the spectacle of a world ongoing a process of decomposition. "The honor, the moral, the Catholic religion, the cult of the family, everything is to be found there, between the legs, everything is to be found there, in the sex, which in Italy is extremely beautiful, worthy of the ancient and glorious traditions of our civilization." (Ibid.).

It is an organic world, infested by all the downfall's rotten odors, like in a dirty night, stinking of excrements and urine, with children trafficked for the soldiers of the French colonial troops, on a stage animated by the city's female dwarfs. I thus reread, mediated by Malaparte, pages from Günter Grass with the group of actors, dwarf-acrobats, sent to entertain the German troops on various fronts like in a farcical and grotesque requiem for a hopeless world. The reader notices the same type of reflexive discourse, enriched by the numerous intertextual references, often extended and blended to reach a tedious state: "Pendino di Santa Barbara is famous for the female dwarfs living there. They are so small that they can barely reach the knee of an average-height person. They are sloppy and vulgar, maybe the ugliest dwarfs in the world. In Spain there are very beautiful dwarfs, well proportioned, with balanced features. [...] The dwarfs in Pendino di Santa Barbara are terrifying and all of them, even the young ones, look like very old hags, with wrinkled faces, with high foreheads, with sparse hair, discolored in tufts" (Ibid.). The purpose is, according to the same narrative intertextual mechanism typical of the reportage (the commentary augments or focuses through hyperbole), to concentrate in the commentary on a main theme with essential value and significance: "Who goes up the stairs in Pendino di Santa Barbara for the first time looks like Gulliver in Lilliput, an intimate of the Court in Madrid among the dwarfs of Velasquez, the foreheads of the female dwarfs is ridged by the same deep wrinkles that dig the foreheads of Goya's frightening old hags" (Ibid.).

For Malaparte, the plague is the symbol of this inexorable unraveling and of the desperation later metamorphosed in a world populated by those who, arrived at the gates of the Inferno, know that they have no escape anymore. The narrator experiences the cynicism with some sort of bitter voluptuousness and charges his eyes with the most hideous scenes. This is the hallucinating chapter entitled "The Wigs", the chapter of the inverts seen in a ceremony which seems to be protected by pre-Raphaelites, by Dante Gabriel Rossetti or Oscar Wilde, by the artists of the Paris evoked by Hemingway or by Gertrude Stein, the city illuminated by Proust's prose and by that which Curzio Malaparte expressively names "the Stravinsky-like transcription of Proust's prose...". The Ephebs converted to Marxism, out of a snobbism not less ostentatious than that of the old readings of Lautréamont, Barrès, Rainer Maria Rilke, Cocteau, Proust, Gide etc., belong to the same city combed by the plague signs. In Malaparte's novel there is the same pathos encountered in the works of Günter Grass or of the German inter-war novelists: the recollection, the torturing recollection of the horrors. The correspondences are inscribed in the recollection's volutes, in the perfect mastering of the flash-back technique. The scene of the Hamburg bombing by the American air forces, the massacre provoked by the phosphorus bombs, the thousands of people burning like torches call for a different circle of Dante's Inferno, unimaginable in the vision of the Florentine.

Such numerous and hard-to-forget moments, are also narrated in *Kaputt*, the frenetic reportage of the war's horrors on the eastern front, and make *The Skin* a "complementary" novel with pages not lacking a certain motivational and narrative legitimatization. The novel's chapter "The Flag" is illustrative for the technique of various correspondences, most of which are preserved in the memory overwhelmed by the sight of World War II, a memory *transcribed* in the formula of the discourse typical of the reportage from *Kaputt*. The novel reconstructs the moment of the Allied troops' "spectacular" entry in Rome, a memorable and significant event. Furthermore, I believe that the intertextuality and the unpredictable transitions from one text to the other could justify the association with another writer mentioned in these pages: Céline.

The "plague" could also have other transformations, names and, of course, other manifestations; it is present in the works of the Russian writers of impressive artistic conscience (I hope it includes another expression of the conscience of dignity and suffering as well), creations dedicated to the inferno of the Stalinist communism (the technique of the suppression of human lives or the mechanism of isolation and the camps were no different during the Nazi or the communist regimes!), dedicated to the attempt of subjugating the people and destroying the human dignity; on the other hand, the spectacle of the West, of the collaborationism (thriving especially in France), of signing a pact with the savageness and the denouncement etc. take up a large space in the confession literature. It would be wrong to invoke literature only as a potential witness in front of the moral courts; literature exists through itself, but Time (History) and the people's destiny in a utterly shaken Europe could not have been eluded by creation.

There are many connections between Malaparte and Céline regarding a morbid, shocking, terrifying vision. I am not (for now) interested in their biographies, in their opinion and artistic vision fluctuations. (In the French edition of the novel (*La Peau*, Denoël, 1968; p. 7-10), there is what I consider to be an extremely significant text, "Letter to the French companions from 1914-1918", a confession and short biography mainly of Céline's literary career.) However, I am sure that Céline, dragged by the events all the way to Germany in the pathetic community of the Vichy government, sheltered in the no less pathetic Hohenzollern castle in Siegmaringen, is connected to Malaparte given the nature of the discourse. The adventure, with its humilities, is no less related to the plague and the inferno from Naples; both writers have the vocation of the nightmare-like representations, of the everlasting transition to decomposition and death.

Maybe the essential meditation, the prevailing feature of the analyzed books, is that of a continent facing dangers just reaching the decisive edging-moment of the truth; the postponing or simply the evasion of the questions, as well as the attempt to challenge an infinitely more cruel and desperate reality than the one lucidly examined by philosophers are the motifs of a literature indissolubly linked to these themes generally valid for the creator. In spite of the aesthetic vision's nature, the accepted criteria for the status of the work of art, in spite of our suspicion of the writers' standpoints, the work in itself is the only one able to account for the illusions, the utopias, the convictions or the doubts of the writer. And the great literature does not necessarily analyze, decanting that which does not belong to the organic act of creation; ignoring everything that is *outside* the creative act, but it responds only to reveal destinies and manifestations of the ontology there where History keeps asking itself, crippled and useless.

A chapter from *The Skin* has for today's reader a special significance and an emblematic value. I am talking about chapter VII which focuses on the dinner given by the American general Cork. Malaparte's commentary springs from the traditions of the European literatures of the XVIII and XIX centuries. It is like an indirect eulogy of our awfully tested continent, often infirming its own values, contradicting them even, but – let's never forget it – maintaing the culture's enduring signs, as writes Malaparte: the cathedrals, the poems, the music, the museums, the libraries, the art galleries, everything that is restless and incomprehensible for the people of the other continents. However, I believe that Malaparte's message has an infinitely greater value if we relate the elegiac accents to everything that the amnesias of the European nations, often dragged in the world of the caverns, meant and still mean... With his lucid spirit, scientific really, extremely thorough and at the same time profound, Musil examined more than an empire mined at its foundations. He set the diagnosis behind a Platonic *anamnesis* for the diseases of the world, of the consciences, of the destinies. Broch did the same thing with the strictness typical of the novelist assaulted by the idea and by reflection, and their contemporaries and followers of the world's literatures gathered in a vast colloquium on understanding the human being, the only important one for literature and for the writers' meditation. The XX century exacerbated and exasperated in anxieties and in disappointing expectations. Thus, sprang the literature created in the same spirit of the freedom of ideas and the questions raised about the people's fate.

Kaputt, the reportage-poem of representations which I believe that have entered the densest and most open areas of the imaginary, the creation of an observer tempted to convert *perceived scenes* into vast poems of beauty or death, of the ghettoes or of the frozen waters of the Ladoga Lake, of the artic North Pole, astonishingly integrates in the structures of Malaparte's novel.

The obsession of the defeat, of the moral defeat (cf. Eugen Uricaru, "Foreword" to Curzio Malaparte, *Pielea*, Bucharest, Univers, 2000; pp. 5-6) is pregnant and it confers that *dramatic* quality reached in an unbalanced register in *Kaputt*. One scene from *The Skin* is fascinating, the visualization and the representation aimed at rendering *the sight* sensitive. It is the chapter "The Flag" in which the narrator remakes, just like a reporter, the scenario of the Allied troops' entering Rome. Each name discharges cultural referents contrasting later with the related scene: the St Peter's Cathedral, the Gandolfo Castle, Horatio's poems, the Forum, the paintings of Poussin or Claude Lorrain ("looking at Rome in the distance, and I cried"), Stendhal, the Cassino facade and, finally, the soldiers entering the city which thus far has been invoked by various testimonies. A happy man approached the troops, but he tripped and fell under the tracks of an American tank. The comments belong to the novelist hunted by the war's ghosts and terrifying images. The *intertextuality* is always present and the use of pages from *Kaputt* is again significant: "A dead man is a dead man. He is nothing but a dead man. He is more or less like a dead dog or a dead cat. Several times, during my trips to Serbia, Bessarabia or the Ukraine, I happened to see a dead dog crushed in the mud on the road, crushed under a tank's tracks. The figure of a dog drawn on the road with red pencil. A carpet of dog skin. / In Iampol, on the Nistre, in the Ukraine, in July 1941, I happened to see on the dusty road, right in the centre of a village, a carpet of human skin. He was a man crushed under a tank's tracks. [...] The Jews wearing black caftans, armed with spades and picks, collected the dead, abandoned by the Russians in their village. Sitting on the threshold of a destroyed house, I was watching the soft and transparent fog that was rising from the shores of the Nistre and in the distance, on the other side, beyond the turn of the river, I could see, slowly rising to the sky, black clouds of smoke: the houses of Soroca. Like a red wheel, the sun was rolling in a powder whirlpool at the end of the field, where the outlines of the cars, of the people, of the horses, of the wagons could be clearly distinguished in the dusty light of the sunset." (Malaparte, 2000)

In the gulf of the city contaminated by the plague of the moral decay, on the Naples shore, the sunset has different colors and different echoes, but it is as tragic and grave as in the vision generated by the scenes taking place on the eastern front: "The sun was setting and the sea was slowly turning the color of wine, the color of *Homer's sea*" (My emphasis added, Ibid.).

Moreover, the tension and the frenzy of the representations would not have been possible without transcending the reportage and constructing it as a work of the imaginary flogged by a reality and a cruelty beyond comparison to anything else. Like the writers quoted in this book, Curzio Malaparte is a cynic, a skeptic and a lucid observer, willing to reflect and thus defeating inside himself the paralyzing feeling of the uselessness of his approach through a final trust in human nature and in the meanings of the abandoned human existence.

This is the reason for which I conclude this journey with a writer who, to a certain extent, is situated on the exactly opposite position (convictions, anti-Semite polemics, disconcerting and inexplicable attitudes), a creator of true value, difficult to ignore within the space of the XX century great novel: Louis-Ferdinand Céline. *Journey to the End of the Night* and *Death on Credit* (or, *Death on the Installment Plan*), works of a strong personality, of a deeply original personality for the evolution of the novel during the 1940s, could not have predicted the evolution of the writer, a tormented human being, tortured by obsessions, by prejudices difficult to understand today, a contradictory and unpredictable man. There is a note dating from 7 December 1941 in Ernst Jünger's *Paris Diaries*: "[...] big, bony, robust, rather heavy but lively during discussions or, more accurately, during monologues. He speaks with his look turned to himself typical of the maniacs, sparkling from cavern depths. He doesn't look either to the right or to the left; he gives the impression that he set out for a unknown target. «Death is always next to me» - and he points to the spot next to his chair as if he was pointing to a puppy that was there. [...] It was enlightening to me", the German writer goes on with his description, "to listen to him getting upset for two hours because in his words twinkled the giant force of the nihilism" (*Paris Diaries*). The analytical "file", actually a cold portrait, lacking any sympathy for "Merline", as he calls him (for the time being) in the quoted fragment, continues with other observations, extremely exact and remarkably intuitive: "It is strange to see how such spirits talk about science, about biology for instance. They use it like the Stone Age people; they turn it into a means to kill the others." (Ibid.) Another note (April 1943) completes the records with other information and other reasons for Jünger's evident lack of sympathy for Céline. One observation of the author of the *Diaries* is indeed relevant; he recounts very somber and sinister cases and situations, most of which are affected by the obsession of the plague: "Regarding this issue, Céline told us about various things from his experience, which seems to distinguish itself through an accumulation of sinister cases. Furthermore, he is from Bretagne – that confirms my first impression according to which I placed him in the Stone Age" (Ibid.).

I once mentioned the "German trilogy" by Céline; I believe that the first volume, *Castle to Castle*, is the most significant given the adopted literary formula. It is true that this formula is present in the next two novels as well, but nevertheless the first book has the merit of a concentration and tension strongly expressed with a desperate voice, charged with resentments, frustrations and trying, at the same time, to absolve and to justify himself even though, it is a known fact, the writer's biography is far from giving the vaguest explanations. However, it remains the important confession of a great and undoubtedly talented writer and the deposition of a writer rejected, to some extent, by history and its gravest events. Actually, it is the history of a nation defeated by its own infirmities, detected paradoxically by Céline and by his contemporary writers.

The trilogy's first novel gives a definite and comprehensive form to an epic discourse dominated by a monologue of strong oral expressions; the exclamation is always present; the phrase is fragmented, interrupted, it requires the ellipse and the breakup of the narrative sentence to finally end with protests and revolt accents. "I haven't forgotten a thing" (Louis-Ferdinand Céline, *Castle to Castle*, Dalkey Archive Press, 1997; p. 10) is the main motif of this agitated, exasperated, fierce discourse, re-collecting and re-determining, according to the narrator's opinion, the truth and not forgetting for a moment to attack Sartre in a recurrent dispute, associating the manes of Mauriac and Claudel, apologizing to the reader for these numerous digressions, repetitions, settlements etc.

Céline, the writer of the 1940s novels, is now the voice of a frustrated human being, hiding, I believe, the feeling of his own errors, failures and compromises, but also proclaiming his awareness of his own unyielding value. The writer has an amazing lexical inventivity; he is incessant and uncontainable, avoiding obstacles and annihilating improvised barricades: "I apologize for talking about myself... I'm overdoing it... troubles?... you have your own!... these literary men are the limit... so afflicted with me-me-ism!... and what about doctors! Just as bad!... and plumbers?... and barbers?... all the same... no modesty... and cabinet ministers?... and Abbé Pierre, the one-man movie?... I keep thinking of Charon... The way he'll knock the me-me-ism out of them! the whole crew! with his blessed oar full in the snout!" (Céline, 1997, p. 18.)

The phrase is totally frenetic; the referents accumulate, agglomerate; a true panoptic imbued by poison is composed in a concentrated manner and the journey to the Inferno in Siegmaringen incites; the eruption of the vocabulary, the information infiltrated as referents of the oral, monologue-like discourse appear as a terrible storm with torrential overflows of words, exclamations, interjections and curses. Céline is even now a creator caught in this inventive and extraordinary mechanism, generating thus an alternative to the novel of balanced, rational, lucid, controlled meditation, although even in this book the cruelty of the insight is ever-present. Is it that "great bonfire of my manuscripts?" (Ibid., p. 38). This is how he names it in the same monologue – a suggestive phrase for the total combustion of the narrative voice. The war, the adventure of the journey to Siegmaringen, the group of refugees make up a picture composed of the segments of this world-ending: "what we went through! deluge on deluge... A little worse that the Théâtre du Châtelet, I assure you!... real flames, real bombs, take it from me! [...] Göttingen, Cassel, Osnabrück? who gives a damn... Any more than about Trebizond or Nantes!... cities that might just as well have burned for two hundred years more... And Bayeux! and Baku!... and why not Naples? All burning... *pot-au-feu* with all the punks in them! meat! guts! vegetables!... speeches, tremolos and statues, blablablah... roll the drums! Troubles, never see the end of them!..." (Ibid., p. 33)

Captives of the word invasion, the transmitted currents make suggestions via these shouted words; they transmit beyond dissimulative elements the tragic of the wasted life, the lucid conscience of the disaster and that inexpressible humility in front of evil. The ostentation, the violence of the language cannot hide a human being that is vulnerable now, and guilty. It is a journey to hell repeated later in the other two novels of the trilogy: narratives which extend the ordeal of the journey through a Germany in ruins, defeated long before the Nazi dementia had been definitively subjugated. It is the journey of the humility and maybe of the expiation, although the narrator tries to maintain, ostentatiously, the impression of potential justifications.

Furthermore, Céline thoroughly follows his polemist vocation and his essential aggressiveness in *Castle to Castle*; despite his difficult-to-forgive-and-forget past, Céline is a great writer and he joins the XX century novelists, traumatized witnesses of the events, the crimes and the suffering endured by the people. Of course, the aggressed and aggressive self of the narrator is always in the position of a victim, a victim who lives his surrenders and failures in the subconscious. This explains his reaction to the surrounding world: "I never want anything... I refuse everything... I don't want a kiss... and I don't want a napkin... *I want to reminisce*... I want to be left alone... that's it... my *memories*... all the circumstances... that's all I ask... I live more on hat-red than on noodles... but genuine hatred... no cheap imitation... and gratitude?... never mind... I'm chock-full of that... Nordling who saved Paris wanted to get me out of the clink... History, take note!... either you are a memoirist or not..." (My emphasis added, ibid., p. 111)

The memory is always called upon; the use of memory and the violence of the language are the factors summoned to preside the universe imagined by the novelists of a generation seriously tested during the pre-war years and subsequently captives of terrifying information about the unthinkable inferno of the extermination, of the death and of the prediction of a new Apocalypse. For Céline, the story of the "1,142" French evacuated in that "that goddam cradle of the Hohenzollerns" (Ibid., p. 125) becomes a nightmare adventure; another Court of Miracles is depicted for a new Dante's inferno: "All pretty miscellaneous! I read it over... How can I expect you to understand all this... not to lose the thread... [...] all for you... getting my memories together... I need the fever to boil me up... To put the details in place... and the dates... I don't want to mislead you..." (Ibid., p. 127)

There is in this monologue converted more pointedly into confession (a confession of the regrets and of the conscience of the faults) an explanation in an assertion able to legitimize this delirious, frenetic, frustrating and suffering monologue. It is the desperation and the humility of the conscience of an authentic creator like Céline. The status of the puppet government and of the refugees is a matter of the refugees' deplorable reality, but it is a matter of fiction. And, it is actually the fiction which saves in the memory of the writer this lost and pathetic world: "The Chancellery of the Greater Reich had worked out a certain mode of existence for the French in Siegmaringen, neither absolutely fictitious nor absolutely real" (Ibid., p. 262). Actually, *Castle to*

Castle is a carnivalesque story, sometimes farcical, but most of the times grotesque and tragic. Just the way the story of the defeated is.

The books of Louis-Ferdinand Céline are the story of an adventure and of a journey. It is the journey of a pilgrim tormented by doubts and conscious of his own faults. And no different from the "drummer" Matzerath imagined by Günter Grass or the liaison officer Curzio Malaparte. The auctorial narrator and, overwhelmingly, the actorial narrator of the German trilogy is a clown and a witness as well; the first, a suffering gnome lead from behind by the war's marks; the latter, a skeptic and a cynic, a traveler through the inferno of the "plague" in the Naples where there are both the neighborhood of the Virgin and the neighborhood of the female dwarfs of unbearable ugliness. Céline's narrator travels through Germany (in *North* and in *Rigodoon*) or through the Inferno's circles in Siegmaringen.

It is the same overwhelming and obsessive image of death and torture, of the end.

Tthe novelist makes his presence felt in the end of the second part of *Castle to Castle*, substituting the narrator engaged in his frenetic and ceaseless monologue. By reading a few extraordinary pages we return to Céline's first novels, *Journey to the End of the Night* and *Death on Credit*. It is the journey around Germany, 1,200 kilometers long, from the South to the North; a delegation of the Vichy government was to participate to the funeral of a French politician who had been hospitalized in the hospital of the SS units from Hohenlychen... It is a Rabelais-like epic "story"; this time the novelist wins and not only the "narrator" in full monologue play, accumulating, invading and denigrating through his language always inexhaustible and original.

The journey is similar to a picaresque adventure with its vast and tragic carnival; it includes a train ordered by Wilhelm II for the visit of Persia's shah, scheduled for August 1914: "You can picture the luxury! all the Wilhelmian, Persian and Turkish elegance in one! you can imagine the brocades, the tapestries, the drapes, the laces! exceeding Laval... divans, sofas, pufuri of leather with reliefuri! And the carpets!... the thickest! super-Buhara!... super Indies!... drapes weighing a ton with brizbizuri!... oh, they didn't care about expenses!" (Ibid.) However, the journey takes place according to the laws of the fabulous and farcical story, with the image of the bombed towns and with kilometers of exposed muslin, with the absolutely grotesque ceremony of the funeral, with the flag prepared to be offered to the Marshal, with a group of children and pregnant women, refugees from Danzig and from Könisberg... The images develop like demented sequences, rolling down through the details' deformation; everything is busy, recorded - the effect is truly unusual, devastating -, and defined within the ascension of the flowing words; and suddenly we recall the image composed by Günter Grass in *The Tin Drum*, in scenes relatively linked due to the heterogeneous accumulation of objects, people, views etc. These are the terrorized people from Danzig at the moment of the arrival of the Soviet troops or the refugees from "Wilhelm Gustloff" embarked for death. Céline brings in his trilogy the singular, distinctive image of his undomesticated verb, flowing like the lava of desperation and of never-ending fears.